joanna morg

presents

THE THINGS GOOD MEN DO

by Dan Muirden

Old Red Lion Theatre
27 March – 21 April 2007

THE THINGS GOOD MEN DO

by Dan Muirden

Cast

JOE	**Samuel James**
NICK	**Tom Harper**
RICH	**Alexander Warner**
LUCY	**Victoria Shalet**
ADRIANA	**Susanna Fiore**
COUNSELLOR	**Victoria Shalet**

Director	**Jamie Harper**
Designer	**Signe Beckmann**
Lighting Designer	**Kate Myran**
Sound Designer	**Phil Hewitt**
Producer	**Joanna Morgan**

Production Manager	**Gary Beestone** for Giraffe Production
Stage Managers	**Emily Hardy** **Rory Neal-McKenzie**
Costume Supervisor	**Karolina Kaźmierczak**
Production Assistant	**Dave Evans**

Press Representative	**Sue Hyman Associates** 020 7379 8420
Production Photographer	**Robert Workman**
Graphic Designer	**Wayne Summers**

The first performance of this production
took place at the Old Red Lion Theatre, London,
on 27 March 2007

The running time is approximately 2 hours
(including interval)

SUSANNA FIORE (Adriana)

Trained: LAMDA.
Theatre includes: *Dogfight* (Arcola Theatre/
Union Theatre), *Leonce and Lena* (Tabard
Theatre), *July 22nd Project* (Oval House
Theatre), *subVERSE* (Theatre 503), *Elegies
for Angels, Punks and Raging Queens*
(Brentwood Theatre Essex/Fortune Theatre),
workshop production of *The Things Good Men Do* (Lyric Theatre
Hammersmith), *Phaedra* (John Thaw Studio, Manchester), *Les
Mains Sales* (Director's Showcase: Linbury Studio, LAMDA).
Film & TV includes: *One Thousand Stories* (BBC Sport), *Divine
Retribution* (Abzolute Productions).

TOM HARPER (Nick)

Theatre includes: *Taking Sides* (No. 1 Tour),
Mrs Warren's Profession (Bristol Old Vic),
King John, Julius Caesar, Danger My Ally
(all RSC).
Television includes: *Lewis* (ITV), *Bad Crowd*
(Channel 4), *Poirot, Foyles War* (ITV), *Silent
Witness, Judge John Deed, Holby City* (BBC),
In the Beginning, Jason and the Argonauts (Hallmark).
Film includes: *Surveillance, Blood and Chocolate, Past
Present Future Imperfect, The Upside of Anger, What a Girl
Wants, Living in Hope, Voices Inside, Personal Spectator.*
Radio includes: *What Hettie Did, The Father Gilbert Mysteries,
Focus on the Family.*

SAMUEL JAMES (Joe)

Theatre includes: Granovsky in *The Green
Violin* (Ballantrae), Trout/Elya in *Holes*
(Theatre Royal Stratford East/Riverside
Studios), Archie in *The Shop at Sly Corner*,
Bobchinsky in *The Government Inspector*
and The Bellhop in *Lend Me a Tenor*
(Pitlochry), The Cowardly Lion in *The Wizard
of Oz* (Birmingham Rep), Paris in *Helen of Troy* (Creative
Battery), Marc in *Diamond* (Soho Theatre) and Tim in *Butler's
Marsh*, written and directed by Robert Chafe. In the West End:
Malcolm McGregor in *The Full Monty*, Harry Houdini in
Ragtime, Danny Kelcher in *Peggy Sue Got Married*.
Television includes: *Poirot: The Mystery of the Blue Train,
Rose and Maloney, Battle of Britain, The Bill.*
Radio includes: *The Eliza Diaries, The Franchise Affair* (BBC
Radio 4).
Film includes: *Closer, Psychic Spies.*

VICTORIA SHALET (Lucy)

Theatre includes: *My Mother Said I Never Should* (Salisbury Playhouse), *Fairytale Heart* and *Riven Court* (Hampstead Theatre), rehearsed readings of *The Sugar Syndrome* and *A Bedlam Of Frogs* (Royal Court).
Television includes: *M.I.T., Jonathan Creek, Midsomer Murders, The Quest, The Vice, The Bill,* Harmony Parker in five series of *The Queen's Nose, Getting Hurt, Natural Lies, Goggle Eyes, Love Hurts, Van Der Valk, The Storyteller: Greek Myths, The Girl With The Curl* and *The Giant* for Jim Henderson, *Ball-Trap on the Côte Sauvage* and *Testimony Of A Child.*
Film includes: *Eroica, The Affair Of The Necklace, Haunted, Shining Through* and *The Maid.* **Short Film:** *Every Seven Years.*
Radio includes: *National Velvet, The River, Ballet Shoes, The Silver Chair* and *The Last Battle* (all for BBC Radio 4).

ALEXANDER WARNER (Rich)

Trained: Bristol Old Vic.
Theatre includes: *Container Conversations* (Courtyard Theatre).
Television includes: *Marchioness* (ITV), *Dalziel & Pascoe, The Robinsons* (BBC).
Short Film: *Beached* (Impasse Pictures).
Radio: *Blue Remembered Hills.*

DAN MUIRDEN (Writer)

Theatre: This is Dan's first full-length play. His one-act piece *Lovely Couple* was shortlisted for Soho Theatre's Westminster Prize.
Television includes: episodes for BBC's *Doctors.* He is currently developing a drama series with Endemol.
Radio includes: *A Fare To Remember* (BBC7).

JAMIE HARPER (Director)

Originally from Northern Ireland, Jamie studied English at the University of Sheffield. He spent two years in America directing at various theatres including the Actors' Studio in New York and the Boston Directors' Lab. He then returned to the UK to train on the directors' course at LAMDA where he continues to teach and direct. He is the winner of the 2006 JMK Director's Award and the 2006 National Theatre Cohen Bursary, and is currently Director on Attachment at the National Theatre Studio.
Recent theatre includes: *The Vanek Plays* (Operating Theatre Company/Tristan Bates Theatre), *The Infant* (Old Red Lion/Gilded Balloon, Edinburgh) and *A Lie of the Mind* (BAC).

SIGNE BECKMANN (Designer)

Signe trained in theatre design and fashion at The Danish Design Academy in Copenhagen, followed by post-graduate study at the Motley Theatre Design Course. She was nominated for the Linbury Biennial Prize for Stage Design and the Jocelyn Herbert Award in 2005.

Theatre: *Scenes from an Execution* (Hackney Empire), *The Infant* (Old Red Lion/Gilded Balloon, Edinburgh), *Looking For My Father* (touring, DK), *A Night for One* (touring, new-circus), *Love in Idleness* (Bristol Old Vic Studio), *Pedro and The Captain* (Arcola), *Breaking News – Rachel Corrie* (Theatre 503), *Blue/Orange* (The New Wolsey Studio, Ipswich), *Tape* (Krudttoenden, Copenhagen), *Pretty Palle* (touring, DK), *Good* (Sound Theatre, London).

Opera: *Albert Herring* (RSAMD), *A Midsummer Night´s Dream* (costume design, The Royal Theatre, Copenhagen).

Styling: *A Portrait of London* and *Kate Moss Liberation* (both directed by Mike Figgis).

Signe has also assisted Steffen Aarfing & Marie í Dali on *The Rhinegold* and *Siegfried* (Royal Theatre, Copenhagen), and Es Devlin on *Salome* (The Royal Opera House), *Carmen* (ENO), *Billy Budd* (Hamburg StaatsOper), *Gadaffi, The Living Myth* (ENO), *La Tito de Clemenza* (Vienna), *Don Giovanni* (Hamburg StaatsOper/The Royal Theatre, Copenhagen) and *Pet Shop Boys World Tour*.

KATE MYRAN (Lighting Designer)

Trained: Kate graduated from LAMDA in 2006 having previously worked in her native Norway.

Recent designs include: *Titus Andronicus* (Mercury Theatre Colchester, Linbury Studio London and The Globe, Neuss) and *Leonce and Lena* (Tabard Theatre). She currently works as the Lighting Operator on the West End hit production *Stomp*.

PHIL HEWITT (Sound Designer)

Trained: Theatr Clwyd, North Wales, and at LAMDA, graduating 2002. He has worked as a Sound Designer all over the UK and abroad, with such companies as Pangaea (Vancouver), and the Peter Hall Company (UK).

Recent designs include: *Dogfight* (Arcola), *Up the Gary, The Whale and the Bird* (Edinburgh Underbelly), *A Wasp in Winter* (Etcetera), *This is your Captain Speaking* (Pentameters), *Blue on Blue, Up the Gary, Futures, Yellowing, Tailor Made Love, The Atheist* (all Theatre 503).

Phil is Technical Director at Theatre 503, and a DJ and musician.

JOANNA MORGAN (Producer)

Recent theatre: *Rabbit* by Nina Raine, Old Red Lion Theatre and Trafalgar Studios (for which Nina Raine won the Evening Standard Award 2006 for Most Promising Playwright, the Critics' Circle Theatre Award 2006 for Most Promising Playwright and was nominated as Best Newcomer by the Whatsonstage.com Theatregoers Awards). *Rabbit* will transfer to the Brits Off Broadway Festival at 59E59 Theatre, New York, from 4 June–1 July 2007.

Other theatre includes: *'Tis Pity She's A Whore* by John Ford, Southwark Playhouse (for which Mariah Gale for her performance as Annabella won the Time Out Award 2005 for Best Newcomer, the Critics' Circle Theatre Award 2005 for Most Promising Newcomer, and the Ian Charleson Award 2005); the worldwide Cheek by Jowl tour of *Othello*; UK tour of *Glastonbury* by Zoe Lewis, designed by Damien Hirst; Declan Donnellan and Nick Ormerod's Academy Company 2002 and its production of *King Lear* for the RSC.

For further information please email
info@joannamorganproductions.com

Special Thanks

Richard Attrill, Tasmin Ayers, Toby Baines,
Breckman & Company, Natasha Bucknor, Adam Bullock,
Central School of Speech and Drama, Bridget Chamberlain,
Peter Clayton, John Cohen, Kirsty Coombs, Rodney Cottier,
Alistair Cramer, Jonny Davies, Jody Day, Helen Devine
and the Old Red Lion, Roanne Dodds, Sarah Fildes,
Alistair Green, Sir Stuart Hampson, Oriel Harwood,
Mark Holmes, Paulette Hughlock for HP Computers,
Mel Kenyon, Suzy King, LAMDA, Penny and Fabrice le Roux,
Ian McAlpine, Sophie MacLaren, Jonathan Maydew,
Luke Mills, Beverley and Pamela Morgan, Matthew Morgan,
Oliver Morton, Richard Nelson, Anna Paolozzi, Neil Ponsford,
Matthew Poxon, Buffy Reid, Heike Roemer, Mark Ross and
Diorama Arts, Ginny Schiller, Dom Slade, Lisa Spirling,
Rochelle Stevens, Wayne Summers, Chris Thomas,
Sadie Watts, Lee Wilson.

and to the following actors for their contribution to the development of this play

Ciaran McConville, Steph Langton, Hugo Cox,
Katie Donmall, Simon Yadoo, Tom Sambrooks,
Claire Andreadis, Ben Smith, Josh Cohen,
John Wordsworth, Rebecca Everett and Em.

**This production of *The Things Good Men Do*
has been made possible by the following generous
sponsors to whom we are extremely grateful**

John Lewis Partnership

U´LUVKĄ
VODKA

A FLAIR FOR THE FINEST FOOD

A Nick Hern Book

The Things Good Men Do first published in Great Britain
as a paperback original in 2007 by Nick Hern Books Limited,
14 Larden Road, London W3 7ST, in association with
Joanna Morgan Productions Limited

The Things Good Men Do copyright © 2007 Dan Muirden

Dan Muirden has asserted his right to be identified as
the author of this work

Cover photograph: Tom Harper and Victoria Shalet;
photographed by Robert Workman; designed by Wayne Summers

Typeset by Country Setting, Kingsdown, Kent CT14 8ES
Printed and bound in Great Britain by Biddles, King's Lynn

A CIP catalogue record for this book is available from
the British Library

ISBN 978 1 85459 994 0

THE THINGS GOOD MEN DO
Dan Muirden

For Jamie Harper

'When the Gods wish to punish us,
they answer our prayers'

Oscar Wilde
An Ideal Husband

Characters

NICK, *twenty-eight*
JOE, *twenty-nine*
LUCY, *twenty-seven*
ADRIANA, *twenty-seven*
RICH, *twenty-eight*
COUNSELLOR, *late thirties*

Location

The action takes place mostly in present-day London.

Note

A forward slash (/) marks the point where one character interrupts the other.

This text went to press before the end of rehearsals so may differ slightly from the play as performed.

Scene One

May 2nd.

A hotel room. Twin beds. Bags on each bed, barely unpacked. Pre-going-out music is playing from an iPod. Both JOE *and* NICK *are in their boxer shorts, in the middle of dressing.*

JOE *has his eyes shut and spins a globe of the world.*

His playful charm can make even the most shocking comment sound amusing.

He stops the globe and points.

JOE. So have I ever shagged a girl from . . . (*Opens his eyes and reads.*) Canada?

NICK (*beat*). Yes.

JOE. Met where?

NICK. In Clapham Grand.

JOE. Hair?

NICK. Blonde in a bob.

JOE (*reluctantly*). Too bloody easy.

NICK. Come on! Three out of three again!

JOE. Name bonus?

    NICK *thinks hard, then shakes his head.*

Her name, and you're going to kick yourself, was Eunice.

NICK. Oh my God, that's right. Damn!

JOE. Twelve–nine. Final round.

He hands the globe over to NICK.

NICK. All three needed. No pressure, mate.

    NICK *shuts his eyes, spins the globe and points.*

Have I slept with a girl from . . . (*Opens them.*) Ukraine?

JOE. Ukraine. Ukraine. Ooh, now the girl you met at that Millennium ball. I think she was from Ukraine, but she might have been from Russia. Dark hair, sort of startled face. Now I know you snogged her –

NICK. She was an attractive girl.

JOE. – but I can't remember if you . . . did . . . the . . . deed –

> JOE *tries to read* NICK.

> – or whether she was Russian. Thing is, I remember her name was Anna –

NICK. Interesting.

JOE. – which means the name bonus is potentially on.

NICK. I'm very confident about this.

JOE. But am I only remembering that because at the time I was thinking of Anna Karenina which would make her Russian, not Ukranian?

NICK. I'm going to have to hurry you.

JOE. All right . . . Come on, Joe. Was she Ukraninan? Yes. And did you shag her? Yes!

NICK. Your final answer.

JOE. Final answer.

NICK. Well, she was Ukranian but . . .

> *Beat.*

JOE. You shagged her.

NICK (*in defeat*). I shagged her.

JOE (*euphoric*). Oh yes. It's there. Stoppage-time winner. (JOE *dances around the room.*) And Joe Rickett takes the 'Multicultural London Appreciation Society Trophy' yet again.

NICK. I can't believe you got the name.

JOE. Course I did. It's because I care. So on a scale from one to ten, how single are you tonight? I should point out that I score ten and a half.

> *They have both started to get dressed again.*

NICK. Well, I'm a bit less than that.

JOE. Come on, stag-weekend rules. It all goes in the vault.

NICK. I'll just enjoy the view this time.

JOE. What?

NICK. But as your wingman I'll see what I can line up for you because I know how you clam up.

JOE. Right. So how is Lucy?

NICK. Good. She's good. It's going well.

JOE. She seemed like a nice girl.

NICK. Yeah.

JOE. And you two seemed to get on OK.

NICK. Yeah, it's good.

JOE. That's it?

NICK. Yeah.

JOE. Have you?

NICK. I'm not saying.

JOE. Right. (*Moving on.*) So when's Rich's wedding?

NICK. Second week in December. Didn't you get a save-the-date thing?

JOE. Clearly not.

NICK. Oh. It's . . . I'll check. I'm sure you'll get one.

JOE. Why do I suspect I won't?

NICK. Actually no, let's be honest, you probably won't.

JOE (*innocent*). What did I do?

NICK. Your chances probably weren't helped when he turned up at that club with the Black Forest Bear . . .

JOE. Oh my good Lord.

NICK. . . . and you told him she was the ugliest girl you'd ever seen with any of our friends.

JOE. You agreed with me, come on. She had a face like a bulldog licking piss off a thorn bush.

NICK. I've never understood why he did that.

JOE. Mate, don't forget. There are three types of girlfriend. Those you tell your parents about, those you tell your friends about and those you tell no one about. She was firmly in the latter category, but then Rich got confused and thought his friends would understand.

NICK. Yeah, I . . . Oh, poor Rich.

JOE. So what's his fiancée like?

NICK. Sarah? She's all right. I mean, she's blonde, English, posh obviously. (*Positive.*) He thinks she's his soulmate.

JOE. Oh Jesus. 'Soulmate.' Is there a more terrifying word in the English language? I mean, what do soulmates do? Sit next to each other reading novels and comparing newspaper articles . . .

NICK. What's wrong with that?

JOE. 'Cause soulmates don't shag, do they? They just 'hold each other'. If I ever spent the night with a girl and she did not want to have sex with me, I would say goodbye the next morning. Of course that's hypothetical. It's never actually happened.

NICK. You've never spent the night in bed with a girl without sleeping with her?

JOE. What would be the point?

NICK. Bollocks.

JOE. I think you'll find it's true. So is Lucy The One?

NICK. I don't know.

JOE. Well, either she is or she isn't.

NICK. I don't know. Maybe.

JOE. Look. The only reason to get married is to have kids. It's just a matter of finding the woman you want to bear your children. So do you want Lucy to be the mother of your children?

NICK. Wow.

JOE. It's pretty straightforward.

NICK. All right. So what do you think I'm going to say and then I'll say.

JOE. I told you. She seemed nice. But do you actually want her to be the mother of your children?

NICK. Well, er, look, it's early days. And there are rumours of ginger on her father's side . . .

JOE. So a 'no', then.

NICK. . . . No, she's amazing and I . . . yeah, maybe I would like to.

JOE. What?

NICK. I don't know, have a family with her. Who knows? Two boys and a girl. Or something.

JOE. Or something.

NICK. Yeah.

JOE. OK.

NICK. So what do you reckon?

JOE. There is one more question to ask.

NICK. Which is?

JOE. The killer.

NICK. Go on.

JOE. Shut your eyes. Picture Lucy.

NICK. Yeah.

JOE. She's nice.

NICK. She's got a white top on and her smile is just . . .

JOE. Now remember the last time you saw a girl on the Tube so beautiful you said 'Jesus!' out loud and wanted to cry. When was that?

NICK. Mmm. Yesterday evening.

JOE. And before that?

NICK. Yesterday morning.

JOE. Now think about the last time you met a girl at a party and your stomach just dropped when you were talking to her. You tried to be calm, listened to what she said, made her laugh. But inside, every part of you was screaming, 'My God. If I was with you, I would have everything.'

NICK. Lucy. A month ago.

JOE. Yeah, all right, but now remember a man becomes more attractive as he gets older and his choice increases. It's like a Darwinian wet dream. So long as he's fairly successful and looks after himself and doesn't go bald. So the girls who are having this effect on you now will become more available to you as time goes on . . .

NICK. Does that actually follow?

JOE. And bearing in mind that you are having these feelings for other girls already . . .

NICK. Not feelings, just, you know, you see them and you can't help wondering what it / would be like.

JOE. All right. So here's the question: is Lucy the last girl on this planet you will sleep with?

Pause.

NICK. I hope so.

JOE. I didn't hear you.

NICK. I said I hope so.

JOE. I don't think she will be.

NICK. Well, guess what, Joe . . .

JOE. And who knows? Maybe you won't be the last bloke she ever sleeps with.

NICK. Sometimes you are just a bit too cynical.

JOE. When one is in love, one always begins by deceiving oneself; and one always ends up by deceiving others. That is what the world calls a romance. *Picture of Dorian Gray.*

NICK. I'll keep that in mind.

JOE. Listen to Oscar Wilde.

Blackout.

Scene Two

May 9th. A few days later.

The living room of a big Georgian house. It's huge and impressive. RICH is standing with NICK, who is holding two drinks.

RICH. Right, first of all, just don't shag in our bedroom or anywhere in the house, all right?

NICK. OK.

RICH. Goes without saying.

NICK. Rich. Did you come all the way back to tell me that?

RICH. I came back to meet Lucy. Where is she?

NICK. She's looking around your pad.

RICH. Have a little chat with her. Good. Sit down.

They sit.

And . . . stag. How are you getting on?

NICK. Yeah, good. You're sure you want forty people?

RICH. Yeah, forty's pretty good except maybe, maybe fifty, but . . .

NICK. That's a big stag, mate. I mean, that's absolutely fine. But that's a big stag.

RICH. Forty's fine.

NICK. You won't even have time to talk to everyone.

RICH. Well, yeah, a few words. But you know I see this like a cruise ship and I'm captain, I'm more the figurehead.

NICK. Oh, well, in that case . . .

LUCY *enters from the hallway. She's very attractive. They get up.*

LUCY. Hi.

NICK. Er, sorry, Lucy. This is Rich.

LUCY. Hi.

RICH. Pleased to meet you.

They kiss.

How do you like the lovely house?

LUCY. Amazing. Yeah. Beautiful.

NICK. It's a very nice sofa. Is it new?

RICH. Oh it's, er . . . well, yeah, it's kind of trendy, well, apparently, can't remember the name of it, Sarah liked it, five grand, make yourself at home. Sit down. You've got a drink. Good. This is your pad. Both of you. So . . . fantastic to meet you, Lucy.

LUCY. Yeah.

RICH. Nick tells me you work in HR.

LUCY. Yeah, yeah, for a publishing company.

RICH. Pay well?

LUCY. Errrm, yeah –

NICK. It's all right.

LUCY. Yeah, it's, you know, I . . . enough to live where I want to live and . . .

RICH. Where are you living?

LUCY. Clapham.

NICK. Clapham's nice. You know Clapham? North London boy, aren't you?

RICH. I've heard of Clapham, Nick. Actually, Lucy, heard today we might have an HR vacancy coming up at MKPG.

LUCY. Really?

RICH. I can get details to you when I know more.

LUCY. Well, that's very kind of you. To be honest, I love the company that I'm in so, you know . . .

RICH. Are you earning £80k?

LUCY. No.

RICH. So I'll let you know more when I hear about it, shall I?

LUCY. Errr . . .

NICK (*reasserting himself*). And welcome to the world of Rich . . .

LUCY. That's OK. Thank you. I'm very happy where I am.

RICH. Oh. Fair enough. Are you sure?

LUCY. Yes. Thank you.

RICH. Interesting. OK.

LUCY. How are all the wedding plans going?

RICH. All right.

NICK. Lucy's been giving me some great jokes for your best man speech.

RICH. Good, yes.

NICK. Cutting out some of the filth as well, so there's no need to worry.

RICH. I'm not worried.

NICK. How's Sarah?

RICH. All right.

NICK. She sorted out the dress and . . .

RICH. Yeah.

NICK. And the bridesmaids.

RICH. Yeah.

LUCY. Wow. So how many bridesmaids is she having?

RICH (*unconcerned*). I don't know.

LUCY. Oh.

RICH. We need to talk more about the stag, Nick.

NICK. I can do next week.

RICH (*thinks*). Tell you what, let's talk it through now,
quickly . . . (*He reaches for his laptop.*)

NICK. What are you doing?

RICH. Well, basically I've found this piece of software called
'Stag Night' and it tells you how to plot your optimal stag.

NICK *can't stop himself from corpsing,* LUCY *hides it
better.*

NICK. Sorry, Rich. That sounds good. Run me through it.

RICH. See, I'm smiling, but . . .

NICK. You found some software called 'Stag Night' for your
optimal . . . what the fuck?

LUCY. No, it's quite sensible though, the amount of
programmes there are for . . . er . . .

Both wait.

Brides. Er, you know, you know, like . . .

RICH *gets a call, sees the caller's name and leaves.* NICK
and LUCY *exhale.*

NICK. / What the . . .

LUCY. He's so funny.

NICK. I'm really / sorry.

LUCY. I feel like such a cow. He's being really kind but when he talks I want to piss / myself.

NICK. I know it's / often like that.

LUCY. He's really nice. Does he always offer jobs when he first meets people?

NICK. No. Never.

LUCY. I like him. I think he's great.

NICK. / He is.

LUCY. And he's so just giving us his house . . .

NICK. Yeah, what an amazing thing to do. / I feel bad.

LUCY. He's clearly just a really . . . he's lovely.

> NICK *toasts*.

NICK. To a first weekend away.

LUCY. To Hampstead. To Rich.

> *They drink, then just smile at each other.*

> So here we are. (*Beat.*) Sorry, but this is the most uncomfortable sofa . . .

NICK. It's all right, it's a bit . . . oh, (*Laughs.*) yeah, no, maybe . . .

LUCY. And this place.

NICK. Yeah, what d'you think?

LUCY. I think four floors!

NICK. Five. There's a basement.

LUCY. No. We might get lost.

NICK. Spend the weekend looking for each other.

LUCY. I'll keep my phone on just in case.

NICK. OK.

LUCY. It's impressive.

NICK. You like it?

LUCY. It's a tiny bit too grown-up for me.

NICK. Yeah.

LUCY. No one I know has got a staircase yet.

NICK. It makes me feel like a bit of a kid being here.

LUCY. Sort of naughty.

NICK. Yeah.

Beat. LUCY *picks up a photo frame.*

LUCY. Ah. They look really sparkly.

NICK. It's a very good photo.

LUCY. How are they together?

NICK. They're all right. They're a power couple.

LUCY. What does that mean?

NICK. They march around. Taking up a lot of space.

LUCY. Rich seems like a marcher.

NICK. He flew once.

LUCY. When?

NICK. With a girl named Caroline.

LUCY. When?

NICK. About four years ago. They met on top of a mountain, skiing, and that was it. They just . . . flew. He was transformed.

LUCY. What happened?

NICK. I don't know. She finished it a year later. I suppose she . . . let go.

LUCY. That's sad.

NICK. Yeah. I think it left its mark.

LUCY. Do we march?

NICK. No, we fly.

LUCY. I like the sound of flying.

NICK. You have to fly.

Beat.

LUCY. God.

Beat. NICK *kisses* LUCY. *Loads of passion.* RICH *enters and interrupts them.*

RICH. All right. That was Sarah. Got to go. (*Folds up his laptop.*) We'll sort out a time for next week, Nick. You're OK about locking up and the alarm?

NICK. I'm your best man.

RICH. All right. Lovely to meet you, Lucy.

LUCY. Yes, and you.

RICH. Think about the vacancy, have a great weekend, post the keys through the door. And Lucy –

> RICH *points to distract* LUCY. *As she looks away,* RICH *mimes 'No shagging' to* NICK.

NICK. Cheers, Rich.

> RICH *leaves.*

LUCY. What was he saying just then?

NICK. Not sure.

> *Front door shuts offstage. The house is full of possibility.*

LUCY. Was he telling us we can't have sex in his house?

> *Blackout.*

Scene Three

May 12th. A few days later.

Evening. A bed in a bedsit. The incessant rumble of night-time traffic. This bedsit is underneath the Westway flyover.

NICK *is sitting on a bed next to a girl who looks a lot younger than he is, but they are actually only a year or two apart. She is Mediterranean-looking, has petite features. She just stares at him. There is something very innocent about this girl and an unsophisticated air about her body language.* NICK *is drinking a glass of wine. He occasionally looks at her, but generally avoids her gaze.*

ADRIANA. I bought you a little present. I went to Brighton.

> *She leaps off the bed and produces a stick of rock from a bag.*

It's real original Brighton rock.

> NICK *examines the rock.*

NICK. Made in Blackpool.

ADRIANA. What do you mean?

NICK (*laughs*). It says it here. 'Made in Blackpool.'

ADRIANA. Oh. I'm sorry.

NICK. What for?

ADRIANA. That it wasn't made in Brighton.

NICK. Well, don't be.

ADRIANA. Sorry.

> ADRIANA *continues staring at* NICK. *She lifts her hand up to his face and begins caressing his cheek. After a few moments,* NICK *pushes* ADRIANA'*s hand away.*

NICK. Adriana, I have to tell you something.

ADRIANA. Yes?

NICK. I've met someone who I'm serious about.

ADRIANA. I understand.

NICK. So we can't see each other any more.

ADRIANA. But that's great.

NICK. What is?

ADRIANA. That you've found someone that makes you happy. I'm pleased.

NICK. Good. So am I.

ADRIANA. Have you been going out with her for long?

NICK. A few months.

ADRIANA. And are you in love with her?

NICK. Yes. I am.

ADRIANA. Great.

NICK. So you understand.

ADRIANA. Of course. I know that you are with other girls apart from me. So I am pleased that you have found just one who makes you happy.

NICK. And you realise this means we won't see each other any more?

ADRIANA. I know.

NICK. And that we can't even talk to one another. No late-night phone calls. No texts or anything.

ADRIANA. OK.

NICK. Nothing.

ADRIANA. Not ever?

NICK. No.

ADRIANA. OK.

NICK. So I came to tell you.

ADRIANA. Thank you.

NICK. Anyway, it's not as if . . . I mean, when was the last time you saw me?

ADRIANA. A year ago.

NICK. Exactly. No it wasn't.

ADRIANA. No. It just seems like that. It was seven months ago.

NICK. I was going to say.

ADRIANA. It was the 23rd of September. Italy played England.

NICK. And I felt sorry for you. For losing. Again.

ADRIANA. *Bastardo!*

She mock-hits NICK.

NICK. Ow!

ADRIANA*'s hand floats up to* NICK*'s cheek. She holds it there for a moment.* NICK *pushes her hand away firmly.*

Adriana. I mean it. You can't touch me. You can't do anything.

ADRIANA. OK.

NICK. So have you met anyone recently? Seen anyone you fancy?

ADRIANA. No. No one.

NICK. What about at work? What about that bloke you told me about once who seemed interested in you?

ADRIANA. Ugh. He's so old and disgusting. He's creepy.

NICK. Do you actually talk to people at work?

ADRIANA. Yes.

NICK. And on the Tube. Have you seen anyone on the Tube?

ADRIANA. I think about you on the Tube.

NICK. Don't you see other men and feel attracted to them?

ADRIANA. If I see other men, they remind me of how I feel about you.

NICK. But do you never see a bloke, maybe in a suit or something, and just look at him and get turned on by him?

ADRIANA. Maybe. Very rarely.

NICK. And what do you do about it when it happens? Do you stare at him?

ADRIANA. No. I feel really embarrassed and want to get off the train.

NICK. And do you think about them when you're back at home. In bed?

ADRIANA. No. I think about you. And I touch myself.

NICK. Adriana. I don't get you. You are so pretty. Look at you in this . . . shithole.

ADRIANA. It's not a shithole.

NICK. You're living under the Westway. It's the busiest road in London. What did you have for dinner tonight?

ADRIANA. Pot Noodle.

NICK. Fucking Pot Noodle. You're Italian. You can't have Pot Noodle every day.

ADRIANA. I don't have it every day.

NICK. What's wrong with pasta?

ADRIANA. I don't like cooking. And I like Pot Noodle.

NICK. It's bad for you.

ADRIANA. No it's not.

NICK. Have you been out recently? Seen any films or anything?

ADRIANA. I'm not like you.

NICK. What do you mean?

ADRIANA. Going out all the time. With your friends.

NICK. You have friends. What about the one you said worked in a bookshop?

ADRIANA. I don't see her so much any more. She has a boyfriend.

NICK. So what do you do in the evenings?

ADRIANA. I come home from work. I'm tired. I have a bath. I eat. I go to bed.

NICK. Every day?

ADRIANA. Most days. Except when I go back to Italy. Or when you come round.

NICK. But I never come round.

ADRIANA. Well, when you do.

NICK (*angry*). Well, I won't any more.

ADRIANA. I know.

Pause.

I went back home for Easter. I've got some photos. Do you want to see them?

NICK. Let me guess. Of your family?

ADRIANA. No, I took some specially for you.

ADRIANA *leaps off the bed again and produces photos from a drawer. She returns to the bed and holds them so* NICK *can't see them.*

When I was at home I was going through my things. And I found this box with all my old school things. All my books. And there was my old school uniform. So I tried it on. And it fitted me. It still fitted me. And I stood in front of the mirror and looked at myself and I thought about you. And so I took some pictures.

NICK. Of yourself.

ADRIANA. On a timer.

ADRIANA *looks at one of the photos. She smiles and slowly turns it to face* NICK. NICK *grabs the photo and looks at it.*

It's nice, isn't it? I thought you would like it. It still fitted me.

NICK. You shouldn't have done this.

ADRIANA. Why?

NICK. Because it's wrong. It's wrong to do this. To take pictures of yourself looking like this. Very bad. You are . . .

ADRIANA. Yes?

NICK *pulls* ADRIANA *to him and kisses her quite aggressively. After a few seconds she places her hand between his legs.* NICK *grabs* ADRIANA's *hair and begins to push her down towards his crotch.*

Blackout.

Scene Four

July 11th. Two months later.

Warm summer evening. The boys sit at a table outside a bar on the street. Latin music can be heard from inside. They are playing 'That's My Girlfriend', clocking girls as they walk past. Each must claim one of the first ten to pass as his 'girlfriend'.

JOE. No.

NICK. No.

BOTH. No.

JOE. What's that? Six.

NICK. Seven.

The boys parody a sports commentary for the following sequence.

JOE. So after all the build-up, after all the training, after all the hype, could it be that the Future Mrs Joe Rickett Championship Hurdle is about to be won by No. 10, who is destined no doubt to be a fat minger. But no . . . wait . . . who's this?

NICK. She's got the walk . . . It's hard to tell with the shades
on, but . . . oh, she's stopped. She's looking in the window
of Jigsaw . . . Ample breasts . . . just a question mark over
the . . . and the shades are coming . . . they're coming off.

JOE. So good of her to oblige this capacity crowd.

NICK. She's turning this way . . . and it's a . . .

JOE. *That* is my girlfriend!

> NICK *and* JOE *watch her go past.*

> (*To* NICK.) You are so slow. (*A wave to the passer-by.*)
> Congratulations.

NICK (*to* JOE). All right. I admit it. You are much better at
'That's My Girlfriend' than I am.

JOE. But it's not over yet.

NICK. I think it is.

JOE. No. She was only No. 8. Two more runners. And you
have to take one or you're on your tod for ever, mate. And
here they come. And one is fat and ugly and the other is . . .
just slightly fatter and uglier. I think they were mother and
daughter, but I'm not sure which one was which.

NICK. What time is it?

JOE (*looking at watch*). She's only ten minutes late.

NICK. She's not late. She's sorting stuff out.

JOE. How do you know?

NICK. She's never late.

JOE. It's all power games. She's playing with your mind.

NICK (*shakes head*). Not this one.

JOE. See, you can't even see it. How old is she again?

NICK. Twenty-seven.

JOE. I guess you can hear it then.

NICK. What?

JOE. The hissing.

NICK. Where?

JOE. From her.

NICK. Lost me.

JOE. I must have told you this one. Hemingway? Or was it Graham Greene? About spawning. Said all girls from sixteen upwards are like inflated balloons?

NICK. . . .

JOE (*sensing a victory*). Right. They're letting their air out all the time. Starts off really quiet. If you have amazing hearing, you can probably pick it up even when they're teenagers. Through their early twenties, you start to hear this noise in the background, you're more and more aware of this hum and by the time they get to twenty-five you can be in no doubt that the air is coming out and they are hissing away. After twenty-five the hissing gets louder and louder, it interrupts your sleep, you can't have a normal conversation, it's there in your mind, sssssssss, until, come thirty, it's all you can hear. It's like having a steam engine in your eardrum. Game over. She's twenty-seven, mate. You're going to have to give her what she wants sharpish before all the air's gone or before you go deaf.

NICK. That's beautiful. Well, I can't hear anything.

JOE. That's because you're deliberately blocking your ears.

NICK. Sorry?

JOE. Mother of your children or run for the hills. That's all I'm saying.

LUCY *enters*.

Ah, is that your last-ever girlfriend?

LUCY. Hi.

NICK. Hi.

NICK *gets up and they kiss. Passionate. Excitement.*

You remember Joe.

LUCY. Yes. We met . . .

JOE. At Tim's wedding.

NICK. Mark's.

JOE. That's right.

LUCY. Just briefly.

JOE. You were wearing a yellow dress.

LUCY. Good memory.

NICK. She looked unbelievable.

LUCY. Thank you.

JOE. I liked your connection.

LUCY. Sorry?

JOE. I was saying to Nick how much I liked your connection. I thought you connected very well. You two.

NICK. Joe.

JOE. I'll get the drinks. White wine?

LUCY. I'll have a pint of lager, please.

JOE. Oh. OK.

NICK. And I'll have a white wine.

> JOE *gives* NICK *a look.* NICK *smiles.* JOE *leaves.* NICK *and* LUCY *kiss and hold a look.*

Hello.

LUCY. Hi.

NICK. How was it?

LUCY. It was fine.

NICK. Yeah? You spoke to Mr Sleaze?

LUCY. It's done and dusted. He'll leave me alone now.

NICK. So we won't have to kill him?

LUCY. No, it's done. It's finished. And I don't care anyway because I'm here now. How are you?

NICK. Yeah, er, oh, Rich, while I remember, I have a message from him.

LUCY. Really?

NICK. Yeah, that job vacancy. They're doing interviews and, well, he can put it a good word.

LUCY. Oh.

NICK. He made me promise I'd pass it on so . . .

LUCY. Wow. Well . . . lots of money.

NICK. It is.

LUCY. But lots of hours too. And weekends.

NICK. How do you know?

LUCY. I did a bit of research.

NICK. Oh. OK.

LUCY. I'd see a lot less of you.

NICK. Probably.

LUCY. My world would shrink.

NICK. It might. It might not. £80k a year. It's got to be tempting.

LUCY. I'd start buying bumpy sofas.

NICK. Yeah, and a massive great Land Rover . . .

LUCY. And talk about changing my kitchen every six months . . .

NICK. And complain about builders . . .

LUCY. And go on and on about 'the area' . . .

NICK. You really want this job, don't you? I'm getting this feeling.

LUCY. Oh yeah.

NICK (*euphoric*). Fantastic.

He hugs her.

Listen, something else happened today. The CEO came in to my office and announced these packages.

LUCY. Packages?

NICK. Yeah, you know 'voluntary redundancies'.

LUCY. Wow. You're thinking about it?

NICK. No, but it just got me imagining. If you had all the time and all the money in the world, where would you go?

LUCY. God. So many places.

NICK. Where would you start?

LUCY. I don't know. A beach. On the other side of the world.

NICK. Let's go.

LUCY (*laughs*). I haven't even said where.

NICK. Doesn't matter. Let's go.

LUCY. What, right now?

NICK. Yeah.

LUCY. OK.

> *They don't move.* JOE *interrupts with two pints of beer and a glass of wine.*

JOE (*to* NICK). White wine for the lady. (*To* LUCY.) Pint for the gentleman.

> *They thank him and swap them over.*

You know, Lucy, I was just thinking. Nick is a modest kind of bloke so he probably won't have told you that not only is he a champion fundraiser for good causes, but he has also won prizes for his poetry.

LUCY (*playing along*). I'm so proud of him.

JOE. For example, he won't have told you about the time he donated his first prize for the 'Save Our Ruddy Duck Haiku Open' to the NSPCC.

LUCY. The RSPB surely.

> JOE's *taken aback.* NICK *laughs.*

JOE. Yeah, I mean the RSPB.

> NICK's *mobile goes off, and as he answers it* . . .

The NSPCC was when he won the . . . (*He thinks.*)

NICK. Hello? Yes. Oh. *Ciao.* Hi. What can I do for you?

JOE (*still thinking*). What would that have been?

NICK. Er, no, not really. Hold on. (*To the others.*) Back in a mo.

> NICK *moves out of earshot. During the following conversation, we see that* NICK *is trying to mask deep discomfort caused by the call. Neither* JOE *nor* LUCY *picks up on this.*

JOE (*triumphant*). That one was when he won the 'Poem for an Orphan' Christmas competition held in . . . (*He searches.*)

LUCY (*playing along*). Eastbourne?

JOE (*pleased*). Yeah. Eastbourne.

Beat.

Nice to see you again.

LUCY. And you, Joe.

JOE. You did look great.

LUCY. When?

JOE. At the wedding.

LUCY. Thanks.

JOE. I think Nick's a lucky man.

LUCY. He's very special.

JOE. Can I ask you something?

LUCY. What?

JOE. Your friend Sophie, from the wedding.

LUCY. Yes.

JOE. She's single, isn't she?

LUCY. Yes. Only recently though.

JOE. I was just wondering if you would mind giving me her phone number.

LUCY. I see.

Beat.

Well, Joe. Now the thing is, she's just been . . . let down.

JOE. Well, what could be better than someone like me to cheer her up? I'm a good man.

LUCY. I wonder. Tell you what. I'll ask her, and if she says yes, I'll get Nick to pass it on to you.

JOE (*pleased*). I meant it.

LUCY. What?

JOE. About the connection.

NICK *has remained still after his call, staring into space for a few seconds. He now comes back over to* JOE *and* LUCY.

NICK. All right!

JOE. Business?

NICK. Yeah.

JOE. Didn't know you were fluent in Italian.

NICK. Sorry?

JOE. Doesn't matter. So, what are you doing for your birthday, champ?

LUCY. We're going to a beach on the other side of the world.

JOE. You lucky people.

Blackout.

Scene Five

July 16th. Five days later.

ADRIANA *is waiting. She's sitting in a park, under a tree. She's quiet. She's been at work.* NICK *turns up. He's just come from work too. It's the first time they have ever met outside* ADRIANA's *bedroom.*

NICK. Hi.

ADRIANA. Hi. How are you?

NICK. I got here when I could. I left work early.

ADRIANA. Sorry.

NICK. Why?

ADRIANA. That you had to leave work early.

NICK. Well, I had to. It's important.

Beat.

Amazing how dry the ground is. Isn't it? I didn't notice it before, but the whole country's turned yellow in about a week.

ADRIANA. Like Italy.

NICK. What?

ADRIANA. Nothing.

NICK. Are you OK, sitting on the grass?

ADRIANA. I'm OK. Are you OK, or do you want to find a bench?

NICK. This is fine.

He sits. Beat.

ADRIANA. So how do you feel?

NICK. All right.

Longer beat.

ADRIANA. I got you a present. When I went home for the scan.

NICK. Uh-huh.

ADRIANA. I'm afraid it's not very exciting. I was a little stressed so I didn't have much time to look.

He unwraps the present she gives him. It's a tie.

NICK. Thanks.

ADRIANA. It's from Milano. It's Dolce and Gabbana.

NICK. Right.

ADRIANA. Do you like it?

NICK. Yeah, thanks.

NICK *puts it down on the ground. He's a bit more nervous now than he was.*

So . . . tell me.

ADRIANA. Well. When the nurse told me the news I was in shock. I couldn't believe it. I was saying that this can't be happening to me. I just cried and cried for days. So I went to Italy to have a scan and spoke to my doctor and basically I had to have tests because it can be really dangerous if you get pregnant after taking the morning-after pill because the embryo can develop outside the womb, it's called an ectopic pregnancy. And then they said that it was fine. But I was doing it all wrong, I mean, I was drinking and eating all the wrong things without realising what was happening. So I was convinced that the baby would be, you know, deformed. Because that can happen too after taking the morning-after pill. But the tests were fine. And then I spoke to you on the phone and told you, you know. And you said it was your worst nightmare. And I was totally in shock when you said

that. I was in tears. I couldn't sleep. It just wasn't what
I was expecting you to say at all. I thought that you'd be
happy. So then I thought about it and thought that it would
be better to have an abortion. Because you were so upset.
So I made the appointment. But then I read about it and
apparently it's common for men to react that way because
they are in shock. And so I thought I would wait until I
could see you. And since then, it's been growing inside me
and I'm feeling different. And the doctor says that I have to
have another scan after four months to check whether there
is any damage to the brain. Because I don't really believe in
abortions but if the baby is brain-damaged . . . But if that's
OK, I want to keep the baby.

NICK (*in shock*). Anything else?

ADRIANA *shakes her head*.

ADRIANA. So how do you feel?

Beat.

NICK (*very measured, trying to compose himself*). How do
I feel? When you first told me on the phone and I said that
it was my worst nightmare, I meant it. And that was a week
ago and that's how I still feel now.

Now it is ADRIANA*'s turn to be quiet. She hasn't been
expecting this either.*

ADRIANA. But why?

NICK. Because it is. It is the worst possible thing that could
happen to me right now. At this moment in time.

ADRIANA. Are you still in shock?

NICK. No. You definitely took the pills?

ADRIANA (*impatient*). Yes, but they are not one hundred per
cent effective.

NICK. I can see that.

ADRIANA. The baby should be fine. I checked on the internet
and the possibility of it being damaged from taking the pill
is really small nowadays.

NICK. You haven't told anyone about this?

ADRIANA. I told my mum.

NICK (*a step further into the mire*). You promised you wouldn't tell anyone until we had a chance to talk.

ADRIANA. You never said that.

NICK. I did, Adriana. I told you not to tell anyone until we could talk about it and decide what to do.

ADRIANA. But I thought you would have changed your mind.

NICK. What did she say?

ADRIANA. She said that it was my decision and she would support me.

NICK. How long do we have?

ADRIANA. To do what?

NICK. To decide.

ADRIANA. In Italy up to three months. So two more weeks. But the baby's already forming now. And I'm thinking that, even though I am still scared, once the baby's born it will be fine because it will be fun. So I think I want to keep it.

NICK. Fun? Jesus, Adriana. Look, you said on the phone that you wouldn't decide anything unless we both agreed it, unless you had my full support.

ADRIANA. No, I said I would prefer to have your support.

NICK. No. You said that you would have to . . .

ADRIANA. Well, things are changing, Nick. It's two months. My body's changing. Why aren't you happy about this?

NICK. OK. I'm going to try and explain. For me, the most important thing in the world is to have children. And for me, this is just how I am, and it maybe sounds a bit old-fashioned, I want my children to be born into a good, loving relationship. Because two people want a child. And because they love each other. That's how important it is to decide to have children. It's the biggest choice we have: who we have our children with and the environment we have them in. And this, this is about as far away from that as you could get. This is the opposite. This is my worst nightmare.

ADRIANA. But now you're exaggerating. I mean, OK, you didn't just see me while we've been going out with each other, but . . .

NICK. Going out?

ADRIANA. Well, while we were seeing each other.

NICK. Adriana. We were never going out. We have never been going out.

ADRIANA. All right, seeing each other.

NICK. We never actually went out. Once. Ever. And we weren't seeing each other. I came round to see you once every few months. When I wasn't with anyone else. That is not the same as going out.

ADRIANA. But you came over on my birthday.

NICK. That was by chance.

ADRIANA. But you said . . .

NICK. Yeah, well, it wasn't true, Adriana.

Pause. This has hit home.

ADRIANA. So do you think you'll ever change your mind?

NICK (*first glimmer of hope*). This was a mistake, right?

ADRIANA. It was an accident.

NICK. This was an accident, a mistake. We should not let a mistake screw up our lives. It's a tragic mistake. But let's not fuck things up.

ADRIANA. But what about our baby?

NICK. We were unlucky.

ADRIANA. But we are responsible for our baby.

NICK. It's not a . . . Look, what happened between us was based on only one thing and that's not enough.

ADRIANA. You think that was sex?

NICK. You know it was sex. What else was there?

ADRIANA. I suppose I thought that there was more.

NICK (*incredulous*). But I never called you except when I wanted to sleep with you. And I always warned you that I didn't want you to feel anything for me emotionally. Didn't I do that?

ADRIANA. Well, now I know it's over.

NICK. What is?

ADRIANA. So now you're saying that you don't want anything to do with me.

NICK. Christ. I never . . . I just slept with you. Very occasionally. And that sex was hardly based on intimacy. Was it?

ADRIANA. For me it was.

NICK. You never told me that. You *never* told me that. Look, I was attracted to you because of your sexual curiosity. You were willing to explore some pretty dark fantasies. That's unusual. It turned me on, I admit that. That you were willing to do that with me. I thought that was what you were interested in.

ADRIANA. But they were your fantasies. You started them.

NICK. Oh no. Don't try that. They were your fantasies. He was *your* dad.

ADRIANA. And that's the reason why you slept with me every time, was it? For two years?

NICK. Yes. Every time. All five times. That's the reason.

ADRIANA. But people in normal relationships have fantasies. Are you saying that's wrong?

NICK. No, but with us that's all there was. And you cannot have a child out of that kind of sex.

ADRIANA. Why not?

NICK. Because there needs to be love. There needs to be a stable and healthy relationship. You can't create life out of . . . that.

ADRIANA. But Nick. The child is here. We are having a child.

NICK. We are not having a child.

ADRIANA. I'm sorry. I'm sorry that you won't be getting a perfect life. I'm sorry that you won't be having the lovely wife and the lovely house and the perfect family. I'm sorry you won't be getting your American dream.

NICK. American dream? It's fucking basic, Adriana. It's the basic thing. A proper family. I'm realising *right now* it's what I want more than anything. Why isn't it important for you?

ADRIANA. It is, but life isn't always what we want. Plenty of
women raise children on their own. It's happening even in
Italy now. Not a lot, but sometimes. And you can get a
house and the government gives you money.

NICK. Jesus.

ADRIANA. My family would support me.

NICK. You want your family to look after you? Adriana,
you're twenty-seven.

ADRIANA. So. It's perfectly normal in Italy. It's not like here.

NICK. Such a great life for you.

ADRIANA. Yes. It's not perfect, but I don't care. Life is not
perfect. But the child is here. And all I can do is be
responsible for it. I feel responsible for it.

NICK. How can you say 'Life is not perfect' when you are the
one who can choose what happens. It's in your hands.

ADRIANA. It's not. I can't do it. I cannot terminate this child.
I'm too scared.

NICK. Of the operation?

ADRIANA. No. Not the operation. That isn't painful. They
give you a general . . . I am scared of the guilt.

NICK. I'm sure it would pass. It does pass.

ADRIANA. How do you know? I know someone who even
though she has had two more children, she still has depression
and she has tried to kill herself because she had an abortion.

NICK. Who was this?

ADRIANA. Just someone. I read about her.

NICK. Look, she's an extreme.

ADRIANA. Maybe she's not.

Beat.

Nick.

*Her hand rises up towards his cheek. He jerks out of the
way of it.*

NICK. Get away. Please don't touch me.

ADRIANA. But why?

NICK. I feel nothing for you. I'm in love with someone.

ADRIANA. Well, I feel something for you.

NICK. Look. I just want you to understand that you will not be the mother of my children. You will not have this child.

Beat.

ADRIANA (*in anger*). Well, I'll think about it.

She gets up and walks off. NICK *waits, uncertain what to do. He goes after her and catches her just as she exits. He grabs her arm.*

NICK. Call me. When you're ready. OK?

Blackout.

Scene Six

July 17th. Following day.

Inside a bar.

JOE. What the fuck?

NICK. Yeah, I'm sorry, mate.

Beat.

JOE. You all right?

NICK. I'm fine. I'm not in the best of moods. I was looking forward to a good night too.

JOE. So why didn't you / change nights?

NICK. He says he wants to talk about the stag and he can only do tonight.

JOE. Well, as long as he doesn't mind me being there.

NICK. We'll surprise him.

JOE. An evening with Little Lord Fauntleroy. / Wonderful.

NICK. He's not Little Lord Fauntleroy.

JOE. You're definitely going to be Rich's best man?

NICK. What? Er . . . yes.

JOE. Why?

NICK. Why not?

JOE. He's just . . . he's just a knob.

NICK. You're talking about my friend, come on.

JOE. You can't be his best man.

NICK. I can.

JOE. 'Cause I think you've only got one best man in you, and that should be me.

NICK. Wait. Have you proposed to someone?

JOE. No, I am lacking a bride. There is that small point. But do you really want to be his best man? I want you to keep your powder dry.

NICK. I know.

JOE. I want you, I want your hundred-per-cent-best best man. I want you to be the very best man.

NICK. It's a practice run. He's a nice guy.

JOE. He's a very nice man.

NICK. He's my mate.

JOE. Is Caroline coming to the wedding?

NICK. I don't know. I don't know. I doubt it somehow.

JOE. I liked Caroline. She loosened him up a bit. I haven't met this new one. The fiancée . . .

NICK. Sarah.

JOE. But she doesn't seem to have helped much. Didn't you . . .

NICK. What?

JOE. With Caroline? After, obviously. I'm not suggesting . . . (*He laughs.*) You being an honourable man . . .

NICK. Didn't I what?

JOE. Didn't you . . .

NICK. Sleep with her? Er . . . .

JOE. Well, clearly yes. Otherwise you'd have said no. I remember. I see all.

NICK. That was, er . . . They'd er . . .

JOE. Rich isn't here.

NICK. Yeah, I know, they'd split up, they'd split up a long long time, two years but I don't, er, it's not something I feel great about.

JOE. Well, it's not something you do to your mates, is it? It's not something you'd do to me. I wouldn't do it to you.

NICK. Good.

JOE. Well, so by that rationale . . . Best man – can you really in all honesty stand up and give a speech?

NICK (*beat*). Fuck off. Stirring things up.

JOE. What? Seriously, I'd feel a bit awkward.

NICK. Don't be a sanctimonious git.

JOE. No, but come on, it's a bit weird.

NICK. What am I going to say? 'Sorry, Rich, I can't be your best man because the thing is, I slept with the love of your life.'

JOE. That would be ridiculous.

NICK. He's got a new love.

JOE. Surely the love of his life is his wife to be.

NICK. Yeah, exactly.

Beat.

JOE. This wedding is built on sand.

NICK. He loves her. He loves Sarah.

JOE. I'm sure he does. (*Beat*.) Hey, speaking of sand and true love, I'm taking Sophie wakeboarding this weekend.

NICK. For a first date?

JOE. Second, Nick. We had a coffee.

NICK. She sounds keen.

JOE. Of course she is.

Blackout.

Scene Seven

July 28th. A few days later, around 10 p.m.

ADRIANA *enters an empty Tube carriage, holding a book. She sits and starts to read. Into the same carriage comes* JOE. *He deliberates briefly, then takes a seat opposite* ADRIANA. *He strums on the arm rest and looks at her.*

JOE. Excuse me.

ADRIANA. Me?

JOE. I've seen you on this train before. Are you stalking me?

ADRIANA. No.

JOE. Oh.

> *Beat.*

> Are you sure?

ADRIANA. Yes.

JOE. Would you like to?

ADRIANA. No.

JOE. OK.

> *After a pause,* JOE *takes it up again.*

> You know. It's a tradition in this country that the last two people on the train become inseparable for ever.

> *Beat.*

ADRIANA. That's not true.

JOE. You didn't see the signs? In the ticket hall. Two silhouettes holding hands?

ADRIANA. Are you all right?

JOE. I'm fine. A little disappointed that we're not getting on better.

ADRIANA. I just wondered why you were talking to me.

JOE. To get to know you a little better.

ADRIANA. Do I have a sign on my head saying 'Talk to me please'?

JOE. No.

ADRIANA. Well. You know?

JOE. Sure.

> *Pause.*

> *Sie sind unglaublich schön.*

ADRIANA. What?

JOE. I was just checking something. You sound Italian but then I thought you might be German.

Beat.

I was telling you I thought you were incredibly beautiful.

Beat.

ADRIANA. I understood what you said.

Beat.

Thank you.

JOE. Don't mention it.

Beat.

ADRIANA. I am Italian.

JOE. I'm good, aren't I?

ADRIANA. You're persistent.

JOE. It was worth it. Just to see you smile.

ADRIANA. *Grazie.*

JOE. *Prego.* Twenty-two. A student at UCL. Studying . . . literature. How did I do, out of ten?

ADRIANA. Zero. I work in a travel agent and I'm not telling you how old I am.

JOE. I'm a dealer.

ADRIANA. I don't understand what you mean.

JOE. I sell experiences to the bored.

ADRIANA. You don't look like a drug-dealer.

JOE. I sell adrenalin. I sell rides.

ADRIANA. Rides?

JOE. Extreme pursuits. Jumps. Bumps. Drops and flops. Dives and bungees. I take people up to the top of very tall buildings and push them off the edge. They want to get close to dying.

ADRIANA. Why?

JOE. 'Cause when they survive, it makes them feel alive. Business is booming. People have never been playing it safer.

ADRIANA. Why don't they just watch television instead?

JOE. No. Why don't they take some real risks? Live a little.

ADRIANA. So what risks do you take?

JOE. I talk to strangers.

ADRIANA. What else?

JOE. I seek perfection.

ADRIANA. That's not a risk. That's a fear.

JOE. I'm not scared of anything.

ADRIANA. I'm pregnant.

JOE. I see.

ADRIANA. So you wouldn't want to be inseparable with me.

JOE. OK.

> *Beat.*

Wasn't me, was it?

ADRIANA. No.

JOE. Just checking. Congratulations. That's wonderful for you.

ADRIANA. Thank you. It's not even twelve weeks yet, so I shouldn't really be tempting fate. But just then I felt like I should tell you.

JOE. You're very honest, aren't you?

ADRIANA. What do you mean by that?

JOE. You are. That's why I thought you were German.

ADRIANA. I'm not really honest. Not all the time. I'm Italian.

JOE. I expect the father's feeling very lucky.

ADRIANA. I wish he was.

JOE. Well, he'll come round to it, I'm sure.

ADRIANA. I hope so.

> *Beat.*

I've just been to see where he lives.

JOE. Was it nice?

ADRIANA (*shrugs*). I didn't go in. I just wanted to see the building.

JOE. I see. And you called me persistent?

ADRIANA *laughs*.

Look, can I ask you something? It's a bit of a strange one, but anyway.

ADRIANA. OK. But I don't know if I'll be able to answer it.

JOE. The thing is, I've just found out something about my best friend's girlfriend. That she probably can't have children.

ADRIANA. That's terrible for her.

JOE. Something to do with her ovaries, you know?

ADRIANA. Does your friend know?

JOE. Not yet. She hasn't told him. I only found out yesterday from her friend.

ADRIANA. Are you going to tell him?

JOE. Well, I thought I was. I've just been to his flat. I spent the whole evening with him. But I bottled it. But I really think he should know. So what I was going to ask was, if you had known you couldn't have kids, when would you have told your boyfriend?

ADRIANA. I'd have told him straight away.

JOE. That'll be the German in you again. Thank you.

Beat.

ADRIANA. Can I ask you something?

JOE. Anything.

ADRIANA. If an English boy comes round as a surprise on your birthday and gives you a present, that means he must care about you, doesn't it?

JOE. Definitely.

ADRIANA. Even if he says that he doesn't?

JOE. He'd be lying if he said that. It's just hard for us English boys to admit we care.

ADRIANA. You're right. Thank you. Sorry.

JOE. For what?

ADRIANA. For asking you a question like that.

JOE. It's fine.

The train stops.

Well, I'm going back to my friend's, so . . . here's where I break with tradition and leave you. Hope it all . . . works out.

ADRIANA. Yes.

JOE pauses by the doors.

JOE. Last chance. Dinner or I pull the emergency cord . . .

ADRIANA laughs.

OK.

He steps off the train.

Blackout.

Scene Eight

July 29th. Following day.

Evening. NICK and LUCY in NICK's living room.

NICK. How was your day?

LUCY. I am so excited. I might have found a flat.

NICK. Yeah?

LUCY. Yeah. I saw it at lunchtime and it's just what I was dreaming of and it's in Battersea, so . . .

NICK. Great.

LUCY. So I've got some details here. If you want to look. What's wrong?

NICK. Nothing's wrong, it's just . . . I just . . . It's . . .

LUCY. What?

NICK. I'm . . . Come on, Nick . . . Why am I . . . ?

LUCY. What is it?

NICK. You can't have kids, is that true? Lucy.

Silence.

Why didn't you, why didn't you tell me that? Why didn't you tell me that?

LUCY. Because I wasn't, I wasn't sure you'd forgive me, I wasn't sure if it was the right time, but listen, come here, come on, stop it, this is all far –

NICK. Sorry.

LUCY. – far too serious

NICK. I really didn't mean to –

LUCY. Please, please –

NICK. I really didn't mean that to kind of –

LUCY. Please stop it –

NICK. – happen the way that it did. It was horrible.

LUCY. Listen. Let's order some food and let's just, let's watch TV.

NICK. It's true then?

LUCY. I don't want to talk about this now.

NICK. Well, I just . . . I don't want to hear this kind of stuff like Chinese whispers. I want you to talk about your life and secrets. I want you to feel . . .

LUCY. I don't want to talk about this now.

NICK. I want to talk about it now. It's important. I can't imagine not being with you and at the same time everything that I imagine in life, everything that I am picturing in some way involves children.

LUCY. Who told you?

NICK. Joe told me.

LUCY. Joe told you?

NICK. He told me because he's my friend and because –

LUCY. Joe told you?

NICK. Apparently it was broadcast.

LUCY. What do you mean, it was broadcast?

NICK. What I heard is that you and Sophie went to yoga together and you were just talking about it like it was like a daytime chat-show or something.

LUCY. Who told you that, Joe?

NICK. No, she just said that . . . it was . . . The implication was that it was no great secret, and that really hurts.

LUCY. I'm telling you, I don't talk about it openly. I stupidly told my best friend because I thought I could trust her and she told her stupid boyfriend who obviously can't keep anything to himself.

NICK. Well, he just cares about us.

LUCY. Right.

NICK. They both care about us.

LUCY. So he just thought they'd storm in and prevent us being able to have a conversation that I knew we needed to have, but I just didn't want to have now.

NICK. Look, they were being clumsy. It was clumsy. It was more than fucking clumsy, it was a bad move. Please don't walk away, please don't turn away. Look, I'm really upset and what I want is just for us to be open so I don't feel like a fool when I'm imagining amazing things that involve you. I'm dealing with this badly because I don't know how to deal with it. I've never been with a girl, you know, where I could get this upset about things before. It hasn't mattered. Hasn't mattered.

LUCY. Well, er, it's, it's not definite. I mean, the condition's / definite but the . . .

NICK. / What's not definite?

LUCY. Not being able to have children's not definite.

NICK. OK, I have to . . .

LUCY. It's . . .

NICK. I have to, I have to understand this. What . . . what . . .

LUCY. Basically all this means is that my ovaries are not quite as perfect as they should be, and that means they have sort of small cysts, or they can be there, it's just they're prone to it . . . It's a bit like having acne.

NICK. You've got spotty ovaries?

LUCY. No. (*She laughs.*)

NICK (*smiles*). Now I *really* fancy you.

LUCY. No, please, please, so it doesn't mean they don't work as ovaries, they're still there. It's harder that's all, it means it's harder.

NICK. So there's a, there's a chance?

LUCY. There's a fifty-fifty chance. That's a lot.

NICK. Yeah, that is.

LUCY. You know that's . . .

NICK. That's good news. 'Cause what I was told was . . .

LUCY. I've been checked by every single gynaecologist, private, NHS, you know, I've done everything I can, everything I can.

NICK. OK. Thank you. That's all I wanted to hear.

LUCY. Sorry.

NICK. I can understand why you didn't tell me. I'm sorry that I freaked, er . . .

LUCY. It's weird because I was thinking, well, either you'll see a future and then you'll freak and dump me 'cause I can't maybe have children, or that's not even in your game plan and you're not even thinking that far ahead, and then you'll freak and dump me. So I was . . . I thought I was dumped either way.

NICK. Lucy. Why would I dump you, why would I do that? What you're saying is that –

LUCY. I'm only saying that . . .

NICK. – in the future there's a chance of us having kids and what we're going to have to do is to have a lot more sex. Is that the . . . ?

LUCY. Pretty much.

NICK. Because that seems to me to be the situation.

LUCY. Yeah.

NICK. So when did you find out?

LUCY. I was seventeen . . . I think it's, you know, I always feel embarrassed, but there are all sorts of factors in life that can stop you, er, having kids or whatever you want to do . . . 'Cause some people just can't and some people never meet someone to love or some people never have enough money or something or . . .

NICK. Well then, we're really lucky.

LUCY. You know? So if you haven't got one of those things stopping you, then that *is* lucky . . . Anyway, that's how I feel.

Silence.

God. Sorry about . . .

NICK. No, I was trying to think of something I could say to that. I feel totally different now that you've told me there's a chance. I've spent the whole day doomsdaying. (*Beat.*) Listen. I think I'm going to take this redundancy package. And then I want you to come away with me.

LUCY. Wow.

NICK. I want my cake. I want to eat it.

LUCY. You're looking really serious.

Silence. Emotion building up.

NICK. I think because actually I'm just a bit of a wreck at the moment . . . Fuck . . . I'm trying to kind of make family decisions and actually I'm just feeling a bit lost. I think . . . I don't know what's wrong with me actually. (*Very moved.*)

LUCY. It's your job. If you're not happy, then that's what happens and it gets too much and then here am I coming in with . . . flats.

NICK. No, no. All of that, it just, everything just, it all just feels overwhelming . . . I just don't know how to deal with it. I'm just . . . I feel like I don't have the facility, like I wasn't actually . . . like I wasn't built to take this kind of level of feeling like this. Oh Christ, Nick, come on. I'm so sorry.

LUCY. No, no.

NICK. You must feel like I'm –

LUCY. Please, please . . .

NICK. Er . . .

LUCY. Please, you're really scaring me.

NICK. I know, I'm scaring myself actually.

LUCY. Please.

NICK. I'm fine. I'm sorry.

LUCY. No, you aren't fine. Don't apologise.

NICK. There's this daydream that I can't get out of my head of you and me just a long way away on a beach and there's not a care in the world and no . . . and we know where we stand. I'm sorry.

LUCY. What's wrong?

NICK. I'm not, I'm not, I wish I could talk about my feelings but I can't.

LUCY. Please come and sit down.

NICK. Wow.

They hug.

LUCY. It doesn't matter what . . .

NICK. What do you think, then? (*Beat.*) What do you think about going away? For six months?

LUCY. I don't know, I think it's something to think about, get excited about, get out the atlas and plot and . . .

NICK. So you think, yes, you think it's a . . .

LUCY. I don't know. It's very sudden.

NICK. This all feels very sudden. This morning, I thought I had this girl I'm head over heels with, who I can never have kids with. This evening I discover that not only is Joe a fucking rhino but there's a good chance I can have kids.

LUCY. There is a good chance.

NICK. So I'm over the fucking moon and I don't know how to handle the emotions. I must seem like such a fool.

LUCY. No.

They both laugh.

NICK. Show me your flat.

LUCY. Oh no. Stupid flat. Oh God.

NICK. Not stupid.

LUCY. Yeah, well. Really nice though. It is nice.

NICK. Paint me a picture.

LUCY. No. It's just a flat.

NICK. What does it look like?

LUCY. I don't know. Brown.

Blackout.

Scene Nine

July 30th. Following day.

COUNSELLOR*'s consulting room. A consultant, female, late thirties, sits in the front row of the audience.* NICK *and* ADRIANA *face her.*

COUNSELLOR. So, Adriana. What made you decide to come in and talk to us this afternoon?

ADRIANA. I don't know. Because there seemed nothing else we could do.

COUNSELLOR. Because you're not sure how you want to proceed?

ADRIANA. No. I think I know but I am not sure. So we . . .

NICK (*confident*). We've been going round in circles.

COUNSELLOR. So. Adriana. What, ideally, are you hoping to get from this session?

ADRIANA. I'm just very confused and want to know . . . I just think I want someone to tell me what to do.

COUNSELLOR. Well, perhaps I should start by asking you what you want to do. Do you think you can go through with an abortion?

Short pause.

ADRIANA. No.

COUNSELLOR. OK.

ADRIANA. I don't think I can.

COUNSELLOR. OK.

NICK. But you . . . Sorry to interrupt. The thing is, that what we really want is to have some different ideas from an

outsider. Because we both feel different things. Because
I fundamentally disagree with the idea of having this child.
And also, Adriana isn't sure. Are you?

COUNSELLOR. Is that right, Adriana? That you aren't sure?
You sounded pretty sure just now . . .

ADRIANA. I'm confused. Because I don't want to do anything
that would hurt Nick. I want to have the child with him,
with his support.

NICK. But that's not going to happen.

ADRIANA. So I don't know what to do. But I don't think I
could go through with an abortion.

COUNSELLOR. If I could just say something here. The
question you have to ask yourself, Adriana, is what could
you cope with? Because if you think that you could cope
with having the child, even on your own, being a single
mother, then that might be the reason to keep the child. This
is what you should weigh up. It's all about the coping.

ADRIANA. When this first happened to me, I was sure that
I wouldn't be able to cope. Especially in England. But now
I am beginning to accept the situation. To believe that I could
learn to deal with it. I would have the support of my family.

NICK. Sorry, can I just say something here?

COUNSELLOR. OK. Neil. Is it Neil?

NICK. Nick.

COUNSELLOR. Nick. So, Nick, you are the partner?

NICK (*slight disbelief*). Yes. Yes, I am the partner. I mean, I'm
not her partner but I am her partner in . . . in this. The point
about all this is that this was a mistake. It was an accident.
It was a really unlucky accident. I think the chances were
one in five thousand?

COUNSELLOR. And you think that this should affect the way
Adriana views it?

NICK. The point is that the most important thing in my life
is having children in the right environment with the person
I love. And Adriana has admitted that this was a mistake
and that she regretted it happening.

ADRIANA. I said that at the beginning.

NICK. Because our relationship was based on . . . well, it wasn't based on anything, it was just physical.

COUNSELLOR. A sexual relationship.

NICK. Yeah. Just sex. And it wasn't normal sex.

COUNSELLOR *looks at* ADRIANA, *who suffers when she hears this and fears the worst.*

ADRIANA. Please, Nick. Don't insult me and our relationship.

NICK. Adriana. That word. We DIDN'T HAVE A RELATIONSHIP. (*To* COUNSELLOR.) Sorry. But I think you have to know the truth.

ADRIANA. Please, Nick. You promised that you wouldn't humiliate me.

NICK. I am not humiliating you. I am telling the truth. So that this person can help us decide what we should do.

COUNSELLOR. I'm not here to make a decision for you, Neil.

NICK. Nick.

COUNSELLOR. Nick. My role is to allow you both to hear what each other really wants. What you really want and once you have decided what you want, what options you are willing to consider.

NICK. Well, what are the options?

COUNSELLOR. Adriana has, just now, spoken very clearly. She has stated – I think I'm right, Adriana – that she does not want to have an abortion. That she does not think she can cope with it. So my question to you is, how much support do you think you can give her if she decides to proceed with the pregnancy?

NICK. I can't give any support. I am fundamentally opposed to us having this child with every fibre of my body. How can I give any support?

COUNSELLOR. Adriana. Have you considered other options? I mean, it's not as common as it once was, but have you perhaps considered adoption?

ADRIANA. I have, but I don't think I could just hand over my child after having it grow inside me for nine months.

COUNSELLOR. And what support would you be asking for from . . . Nick?

ADRIANA. Well, I would not be looking for any financial support. I would just hope that he would be around, to be with me for our baby, to help me through this.

COUNSELLOR (*upbeat*). So how do you feel about that? She has said that she does not seek any financial support from you. So what emotional support do you think you can give her in this?

A beat as NICK *senses that the world is conspiring against him.*

NICK. A question. The reason why Adriana is afraid of having an abortion, why she feels she couldn't cope, is because of the fear of the after-effects. Now I checked. On your website, you state that there is no evidence of long-term after-effects from an abortion. Is that right?

COUNSELLOR. That is correct.

NICK. So there is no evidence that Adriana would suffer any long-term damage from terminating this pregnancy now?

COUNSELLOR. I am not here to tell Adriana whether she would or would not suffer any trauma in the future.

NICK. But surely this is precisely the point. She needs to know this.

ADRIANA. I think I already know.

NICK. Because if she is going to make a decision to proceed with this pregnancy out of fear of the consequences were she to abort, then she needs to know whether the fear is justified. Otherwise how can she answer the question about whether she's going to cope? (*Sensing a victory.*) How can she know if she doesn't have some idea of what she's going to go through? It's all about weighing up fear and consequences, isn't it?

ADRIANA. You say I mustn't decide to have a baby because I'm scared. But what about killing a baby because I'm scared? Isn't that worse? That's for ever.

NICK. Yeah, and having a baby is for ever.

ADRIANA. You are so pessimistic.

NICK (*to* COUNSELLOR). I wonder. Could you perhaps leave us alone, so that I can discuss this with my . . . partner.

COUNSELLOR. Certainly. Is that fine with you, Adriana?

ADRIANA *nods.*

COUNSELLOR *gets up. As she's heading for the door, she turns back to* NICK.

Nick. How long have you known that Adriana is pregnant?

NICK. About four weeks.

COUNSELLOR. Do you think there's any possibility that you are still in shock?

NICK. No.

COUNSELLOR. Ring that bell when you have finished, OK?

She leaves.

Pause.

NICK. How dare you?

ADRIANA. What did I do?

NICK. How dare you come in here and not even discuss it?

ADRIANA. I wanted to.

NICK. You said right away that you didn't want an abortion.

ADRIANA. It was just the way she asked the question. I didn't think I could answer it any other way.

NICK. You didn't even consider the alternative. You didn't open your mind once.

ADRIANA. I wasn't so confused when she was talking. I felt more sure.

NICK *is now in agony. His last throw of the dice.*

NICK. You realise what will happen, don't you? If you don't terminate. You realise that you will be completely on your own?

ADRIANA. You told me. I know I may not meet anyone for a long time. I know it will be harder with a baby. I may not have sex again for several years. Even you don't want to touch me at the moment.

NICK. I'm not sure you understand what that means, Adriana. Completely on your own. That means, goodbye. That means you will not see me again, you will never be able to pick up

the phone to ask me anything, to give you any assurances.
That means that if you decide to do this on your own,
that's it.

ADRIANA. But what about being there at the birth? Or for
scans? I thought you would at least want some involvement.

NICK. I would have *no* involvement.

ADRIANA. But I always thought that you would.

NICK. The only way I would ever, ever be able to deal with
something like this is to completely separate it from the rest
of my life. To cut it off completely. That's what I would do.

ADRIANA. But what about if the baby was ill? Wouldn't you
even leave a number or something for me to contact you?

NICK. Nothing.

Pause. NICK lets this sink in.

That's the reality, Adriana. I'm just letting you know what
you would have to cope with. Because you cannot make the
decision otherwise. That's what the counsellor said.

ADRIANA *begins to sob. Very gently. We have not seen it
till now. She recovers.*

ADRIANA. I have something to tell you, Nick.

NICK. Yes?

ADRIANA. I'm in love with you.

NICK. Oh fuck.

ADRIANA. I have been in love with you for a long time.
I think secretly since we met. I know we only had sex when
we met, but I used to imagine what it would be like to go
out with you . . .

NICK. Adriana . . .

ADRIANA. I used to hope that you would change your mind
about me and want to see me as your girlfriend. I used to
write it all down in my diaries, about sex and you and us,
and I think deep down I did want a child with you. I think
I used to hope that the contraception would not work –

NICK. You stupid . . .

ADRIANA. – and I really thought that if I did become

pregnant, that you would be happy about it and that we would have the baby together. So when I did get pregnant, I was scared but then I saw it as a gift.

NICK. Did you deliberately not take the pill?

ADRIANA. No.

NICK. Answer me, Adriana. Did you deliberately not take the pill so that you might get pregnant?

ADRIANA. No. I promise. I wouldn't do that.

NICK. Jesus. This whole thing's in your head, isn't it? You have no idea about . . . anything. I don't think you know me at all. Once we'd had sex, I couldn't bear to be near you. Remember?

ADRIANA. But sex is a good start, isn't it?

NICK. We didn't just have sex. Normal sex. Do not for one minute believe that what we did is normal for me. God, if only you could have seen how I am with . . . other girls.

ADRIANA. So you're saying that I'm a prostitute? I was like a prostitute for you.

NICK. No, I'm not saying . . . Well, yes, actually I am saying that. You were like a prostitute to me. That's how much you meant to me. Only it was better than that. I didn't have to pay you. In fact, you paid me – you kept buying me presents. I'd go and see you when I could be arsed, when I was bored or when I hadn't fucked anyone for a while, you'd tell me the darkest thoughts you could imagine, turn me on, tell me how much you'd fantasised about me, let me fuck you as hard as I liked, how I liked, and then you'd give me some expensive aftershave or something, and then I'd make up some pathetic excuse and leave. You'd do anything I asked. I didn't have to do anything back. So yes, you're completely right. You were like a prostitute to me. When I left your craphole of a flat and walked to the Tube, trying not to get run over as I went, I would feel a little bit sick inside. A bit like I imagine people do when they have just been to see a prostitute. The thing was, it never lasted. The next day, when I woke up, I'd be fine. And you'd have given me all these amazing stories from your head that I could keep in mine for the following weeks, months, years, whatever.

ADRIANA. I don't care what you think of me. I want to have our baby. I can't murder it. It's too late.

NICK. It's not too late. You can go out that door, book an appointment at reception and have the abortion tomorrow. You could end all this.

Beat.

ADRIANA. I might have been able to do it at the beginning. If I'd known how you felt.

NICK. You can still do it. You can do it right now.

Beat.

They'll look after you here. And all this hurting will stop.

Pause.

ADRIANA *gets up, goes over to the door and rings the bell.*

ADRIANA. I can't. I love you. I want our baby.

NICK *has only one weapon left.*

NICK. Is that final?

ADRIANA. Yes.

NICK. Right – then I think your parents need to know the truth about us.

ADRIANA. What do you mean?

NICK. Well, since they are the ones who'll be supporting you, it's only fair that they know the truth of our relationship, what created the child they'll be looking after.

ADRIANA. But I've told my mother the truth. That I really liked you and that we . . . saw each other.

NICK. Not quite the whole truth, is it?

ADRIANA. So you want to tell them that our relationship was based around sex? I don't think they will be shocked by that.

NICK. No. I want them to know what kind of sex we had. I especially think Massimo should know. What you asked me to do. What you fantasise about. What you've really thought of doing with your dad. Papa. Massimo. Who you really are.

Beat.

ADRIANA. So? I'm not scared. How can you prove that? They'll laugh at you.

NICK. I kept your text messages. They'll print them for a pound at any phone shop.

ADRIANA. You wouldn't do that. You don't have my address in Italy.

NICK. Via Croce. Minnervino.

ADRIANA (*terror*). How did you get that?

NICK. Electoral roll.

ADRIANA. No.

Blackout.

Scene Ten

August 1st. Two days later.

One light picks out ADRIANA *speaking into her phone. Another picks out* NICK *listening to these messages through the answerphone in his flat.*

ADRIANA. I'm sorry to call you at home. You weren't answering your mobile. I'm not feeling too good. I'm scared and alone and petrified. I've been thinking about what you've said and I do agree with a lot of it. I think I will do what you want. Please call me.

The machine moves to the next message.

(*In distress.*) I'm sorry, Nick. I really need to see you. I've booked the appointment in Italy and my flight. I'm going to do what you want. I don't want to see you suffer. But I can't do this on my own. Please Nick.

NICK *registers utter relief. The war is won.*

Scene Eleven

August 1st. Later the same day.

NICK*'s flat.* LUCY *arrives. She is barely in the door and* NICK *kisses her long and hard.*

LUCY. Hello. What was that for?

NICK. That was for you.

LUCY. Thank you.

NICK. You look gorgeous.

LUCY. Thank you.

NICK. Come and sit down. Come and sit down.

LUCY. What time is it?

NICK. Doesn't matter. We'll go soon.

LUCY. Ahhh happy days. It's Friday.

NICK. How was your day?

LUCY. Great, great.

NICK. Yeah?

LUCY. Yeah. Just one of those days where . . . I don't know . . .

NICK. Tell me about it.

LUCY. Just, you know, work was fine and I went for a walk at lunchtime and thought, 'Fuck. I love this city,' you know, and so excited about this flat and . . .

NICK. Tell me about this flat.

LUCY. Well, I think I'm going to take it. I think I could move there and you could move in if you like and we could just start this life of a couple of young twenty-somethings in London, this is what we are . . .

NICK. OK, but let's go away first. Come away with me. To Fiji. I want to see you in a bikini. Come away with me, come away . . .

LUCY. No, no.

NICK. The sun.

LUCY. No, but listen, listen, imagine it, in our own place, all the shops near, like little coffee shops, yoga, we'll have neighbours . . .

NICK. Don't need neighbours.

LUCY. It would be so amazing.

NICK. I want you on a plane right now to Fiji. Right now. Pack your stuff, let's go.

LUCY. Maybe we could go at Christmas or Easter?

NICK. Come on. Let's not plan it. Let's be romantic.

LUCY. I don't want to just leave now, I feel happy and settled.

NICK. You don't want to sit on the beach and soak up some sun?

LUCY. No, I want us to start –

NICK. / And relax.

LUCY. – making plans for the future and and, you know, getting –

NICK. OK.

LUCY. – getting things organised, getting a mortgage, getting a . . .

NICK. Oh. Friday night and we've got a mortgage. Ugh.

LUCY. No, come on, please be serious.

NICK. I am serious. I'm hearing you. I feel weighed down with responsibility.

LUCY. We'd have no more worry about where / we're going to be.

NICK. Could you just pass the sunscreen? I'm just just lying here –

LUCY. Nick . . .

NICK. – on the beach.

LUCY. Get yourself off your beach, please.

NICK. No. Don't take me off my beach.

LUCY. I've got some really serious news. That was all serious, but, er . . .

NICK. OK. What's up? Don't tell me you're going to dump me. You're not going to dump me?

LUCY. No.

NICK. OK. Fine. Anything else I can deal with.

LUCY. Not only have I just found the flat of my dreams and the man of my dreams –

NICK. Hee-hee . . .

LUCY. – but I've just found the job of my dreams.

NICK. Brilliant.

LUCY. Yeah.

NICK. Congratulations.

LUCY. I know. Amazing. Yeah. Fuck. Rich. Would you believe it. Remember that vacancy thing at MKPG?

NICK. Yeah. You weren't interested.

LUCY. Well, I decided to go for the interview anyway and, fuck . . .

NICK. You're at MKPG.

LUCY. I got the fucking job.

NICK. No.

LUCY. I got the job. I'm going to have the flat. I've got the . . . It's amazing, yeah.

NICK. Life is complete.

LUCY. Life is complete. (*Beat*.) / Happy for me?

NICK. Congratulations.

LUCY. Happy for us. I'm really happy.

NICK. When do you start?

LUCY. Three weeks.

NICK. You're fucking kidding me. You handed in your notice?

LUCY. Yeah.

NICK. Jesus, this is momentous.

LUCY. Yeah.

NICK. You handed in your notice today?

LUCY. Yeah.

NICK. What did they say?

LUCY. Fine, it's MKPG.

NICK. Wow, that's a life-changing thing, life-changing.

LUCY. It's going to be incredibly long hours.

NICK. And you're completely happy about that?

LUCY. Well, I think . . .

NICK. It's the life you want?

LUCY. Well, I think if we're honest, it's the life we both want, isn't it? All those things, family, security, great pension scheme . . .

NICK. Well, I want you and I want family, but –

LUCY. I mean, I know we've talked about going away, but sometimes I think people aren't actually designed to just float and it's really . . . I've just . . . I think I've just realised I love this idea of every day up at seven-thirty, get on the Tube, go in to work, be with like-minded people, you know? Get to the office, sit there, know what you have to do, know how you have to do it, it never changes, you can do it, you're in your stride, you know?

NICK. Wow . . .

LUCY. Bish bish bish, I can do it, I'm good. You know? Wwooosh. Out. Twelve-thirty. *Pret*. Tiger Prawn with rocket. You know?

NICK. You're really surprising me.

LUCY *laughs*.

You're joking. You're joking. You're joking.

LUCY. I quit my job so we can go away.

NICK. What!!

NICK *gets up and they hug euphorically*.

I can't . . . Why did you do that to me! Fucking . . . Rich? I thought I was going out with a psychopath. We're going away, we're going away!

LUCY. Yes.

NICK. Oh my God. We're going away, we're going away, we're going to Fiji. Don't ever . . .

LUCY. Oh, I wanted to keep it up but / I couldn't.

NICK. Don't ever . . . What about the flat?

LUCY. The flat can wait six months . . .

NICK. OK, OK, we're going to Fiji, we're going to Fiji – when?

LUCY. I don't know. I quit today. A week?

NICK. We should go, I, let me pack my . . . I got redundancy.
I've got money coming in, we'll we'll go we'll go to the
airport, let's get a taxi . . .

LUCY. No.

NICK. This weekend?

LUCY (*laughing*). We can't just . . .

NICK. We could go to Trailfinders tomorrow, we could get
a round-the-world ticket, we could we could get fifteen
Lonely Planets, we can look on the internet . . .

LUCY. Let's go and . . . let's fuck the dinner.

NICK. Let's stay in. Let's stay in.

LUCY. OK.

NICK. Let's stay in and just get drunk together.

LUCY. Yes, yes . . .

NICK. To celebrate the fact that you are no longer . . .

LUCY. An HR . . .

NICK. What does it stand for again?

LUCY. I don't know, Hell Realised.

NICK. She's beautiful, she's funny and we're going to Fiji.
There's champagne in the fridge.

*NICK leaves. The landline in the living room rings. After
the first ring, it goes straight to answerphone.*

ADRIANA (*voice-over, sobbing*). Nick. It's Adriana again. You
can't keep ignoring me. I need you. I cannot terminate our
baby without your support. Call me. Please.

NICK comes back in.

NICK. Champagne.

It pops as he comes in. LUCY *hasn't moved.*

OK? Hey? All right? What, Lucy Lucy, hey, what's the
matter? Champagne. We're going away. What's the matter?

LUCY *gets up slowly.*

LUCY. I've got to . . .

She disappears into the bedroom and locks the door. NICK *sees there is a message on his answerphone.*

Blackout.

Scene Twelve

August 4th. Three days later.

Daytime. NICK *and* JOE *in a playground.* JOE *holds a football.*

JOE. I'm sorry.

NICK. Thanks.

JOE. I called you.

NICK. I know.

JOE. I knocked on your door.

NICK. I know.

JOE. You could have texted or something.

NICK. To say what?

JOE. To say, I don't know, leave me alone for a couple of days.

NICK. I'm sorry.

JOE. I was worried, you know . . . Sophie hasn't been able to . . . Lucy's not returning her calls either so I've been, er . . . What happened?

NICK. I really don't know. We talked and er, she . . . it turns out she wasn't the one.

JOE. The one.

NICK. Yeah, the mother of my children. It wasn't her.

JOE. Oh.

NICK. She wasn't the one who was going to have my child.

JOE. You sound sure about that.

NICK. I am. I was.

JOE. So it was about all that . . . the ovary thing?

NICK. No, it's not that – oh, it might be, it might be. I don't know.

JOE. 'Cause I was worried about that, that that might be the problem.

NICK. She said to me, you know, I don't want to be with you any more, I said why, she said well, I don't, you know, it's, I don't, I'm, to be honest, I'm not clear.

JOE. But it's weird.

NICK. I know.

JOE. You were great together. You were brilliant.

NICK. Well, that's what I thought, that's what I thought.

JOE. Well, it must be the ovaries, then. So now I feel responsible.

NICK. I don't think you should feel responsible, I don't think it is the ovary thing, I think actually what it is, is she just doesn't love me any more.

JOE. But what's there not to love? Are you definitely sure? Have you spoken to her?

NICK. Yeah. It was a little bit acrimonious, actually.

JOE. Plate-throwing?

NICK. No plates to hand.

JOE. But I don't understand. If she quit her job to be with you and then . . . aren't you're supposed to be on a plane by now?

NICK. Yeah.

JOE. Talk me through it. Talk me through the . . .

NICK. There's nothing to say, mate.

JOE. Come on. There is.

NICK. There's nothing to say.

JOE. There must be something to say. I can't, I can't understand how two people can be so into each other, have all these plans and then in one night have a row about . . . I don't know, I mean . . .

NICK. It was a gradual, er, winding down, an argument, I wish I could be more specific, but it's really difficult. I think what it was is that she got, she got so far down the line and then she actually thought I'm not all that, I'm not all that she hoped I'd be. I've got a small cock.

JOE. She didn't mind your small cock before.

NICK. Well, she never said anything about it.

JOE. She told me she loved your . . .

NICK (*laughs*). It's not that small.

JOE. She said it was her favourite . . .

NICK. All right.

JOE. She said she liked the fact that . . .

NICK. Stop now.

JOE. All right, but I genuinely can't understand why . . . I've seen you two together and I've never known you to be like that with any other girl. I've never known you to be that . . . loving.

NICK. Well, it obviously wasn't enough.

JOE. There has to be something with her which is out of your control, there must be something else in her life that you can't beat yourself up over 'cause it's nothing to do with you. You need to speak to her again, you can't just leave it like this, you can't just sit here.

NICK. I can just sit here, actually.

JOE. You seem to have just given up.

NICK. I can sit right here and I can just feel sorry for myself for a little bit. I don't think there's anything I can do to fix it, or that I should go and speak to her. I don't want to upset her.

JOE. Well, shall I go and speak to her?

NICK. No.

JOE. I don't know, I'm feeling bad and I just want to help you in some way.

NICK. Why are you feeling bad? Ah, Joe. Why are you my friend?

JOE. Why?

NICK. Yeah.

JOE. You're my boy. I don't want to see you down. I don't want to feel like . . .

NICK. Well, what if what if I turned out to be a shit? What if it turned out after all this time that actually I was a disgusting piece of shit?

JOE. Oh for fuck's sake, don't get all . . . You're not a disgusting piece of shit. I credit myself with being able to spot a piece of shit when I see one. I would have spotted a shit-like tendency long ago.

NICK. I know.

JOE. I have faith in my selection of best man. Come on.

NICK. I lost her.

JOE. But that doesn't mean you're bad. I know you. You're a loyal, caring guy who . . . you don't do wrong by people. And that hasn't changed because you just split with Lucy.

NICK. What does that mean, 'Don't do wrong by'? You know? I don't get into fights, but . . .

JOE. I know that if I needed someone to help me, I know you'd cover me. You're an honourable guy, you know, you . . .

NICK. Of course.

JOE. But don't forget that, because . . .

NICK. We do try to do our best, don't we, about things? And sometimes . . .

JOE. If it's the right thing to break up, it's the right thing.

NICK. It's not the right thing.

JOE. Well, it doesn't change the fact that you're a good man.

Pause.

You smiled a lot with her.

NICK. Yeah.

JOE. God, what does it take, eh?

NICK. The mother of your children.

JOE. Well, that's important.

NICK. According to you, that's everything.

JOE. I never actually said that.

NICK. You did.

JOE. Did I say that?

Pause.

NICK. I was in this thing once. With a foreign girl.

JOE. Which one?

NICK. A long time ago. Really casual. And we had this scare. This girl thought she was pregnant. Really thought it. It all worked out fine in the end. But I did wonder, for a few days. Because she told me at first that she would keep it. And I wonder what would have happened if she had been pregnant and gone through with it.

JOE. Well, I guess you would have had a kid.

NICK. Yeah. But about how I would have felt. Because I wouldn't have wanted her to have it.

JOE. Where's this come from?

NICK. All this has made me think of it.

JOE. Don't ask me.

NICK. What do you think, though?

JOE. I don't know.

Beat.

You'd have probably absolutely crapped yourself, hated the girl, hated yourself for getting in the shit, cried lots, not told your mum until the last minute. And then when the kid was born, you would have held it, cried again, and not been able to conceive that you ever wanted not to have it.

NICK. Do you think?

JOE. Yeah. You're an old softie at heart.

NICK. But what if you really don't like the girl? You're stuck to the wrong person for ever with this . . . cord. It would be hell.

JOE. Why? You don't have to marry her or anything. OK, it's not perfect, but I suppose you just get on with it. You can still meet someone.

NICK. How could anyone have two lives like that?

JOE. I suppose they just would. Because they had to.

NICK. All right. But what about meeting someone else? I mean, it's a bit of a conversation-killer, isn't it? 'I want to spend the rest of my life with you – just us two. Oh, and a kid that was a mistake from a previous relationship that didn't mean anything.'

JOE. At least they know you're functioning.

NICK. More like over-functioning.

JOE. You know what's weird about it is that you would now have a kid of . . . how old?

NICK. I don't know. Four? Five?

JOE. Five. You imagine? Knowing that you already had a kid in this world that was yours. That part of you was running around somewhere in Venezuela or Japan.

NICK. Or Acton.

JOE. Yeah. You would already have a lineage. You would already have done what you were put on the earth to do. Sort of takes the pressure off a little, doesn't it? Yeah, that would be . . . an interesting experience.

NICK. 'Experience is the name we give to our mistakes.'

JOE. Did I just get a little Oscar thrown back in my face?

NICK. Yup.

JOE. Ouch. So this happened at university, then?

NICK. Around that time, yeah.

JOE. And you kept it to yourself?

NICK. It was only a few days. It wasn't a massive deal.

JOE. Come on. Which one was she?

NICK. It doesn't matter.

JOE. One of your sly ones.

NICK. One of the ones you tell no one about.

JOE. God. If something major like that was happening in my life, you'd be the first to know.

NICK. I know.

Beat.

JOE. Actually, I have got some major news.

NICK. Yeah?

JOE. I think Sophie might be my soulmate.

Blackout.

Scene Thirteen

August 4th. Later the same day.

On a bench, overlooking water.

NICK. Now that you're definitely going, now that you're sure, it feels good.

ADRIANA. It does.

NICK. Tomorrow night you'll be with your parents, getting some proper TLC. It's an acronym, it means 'tender loving care'.

ADRIANA. I know.

NICK. They'll feed you, pasta, they'll sit you down, feed you . . .

ADRIANA. Probably not.

NICK. Yes they will. You may even want to stay in Italy.

ADRIANA. No.

NICK. Well, why come back? All the beautiful . . . everything . . . over there.

ADRIANA. I like the Westway. And I like the people that I know here.

NICK (*pushing her away*). You must have more friends at home. And your own language and your own sunshine. God, the effect the sunshine today is having on me. If I was Mediterranean, I don't think I'd ever leave.

ADRIANA. No. It's boring.

NICK. Why's it boring? Ancient Rome, the gladiators . . .

ADRIANA. I don't care, I want to be here.

NICK. In that flat?

ADRIANA. Yes.

NICK. You really don't.

ADRIANA. And I want, I want to carry on. I want to just do this week.

NICK. Yeah. This week. Exactly.

ADRIANA. And just carry on. Forget it.

NICK. Yeah. Carry on how?

ADRIANA. Like this. This is nice.

NICK. You mean us carry on?

ADRIANA *nods*.

No way. No, Adriana. I don't want to hurt you any more.

ADRIANA. You don't.

NICK. I don't hurt you? Come on.

ADRIANA. I have to tell you something.

NICK. What.

ADRIANA. I don't know how it happens, but sitting here with you, even when all this is going on, I feel like . . . I can't say it.

NICK. What.

ADRIANA. I still want to . . . (*Whispers into* NICK*'s ear.*)

NICK. Adriana.

ADRIANA. It's true.

NICK. No . . . I'm in a relationship.

ADRIANA. Yeah, but. You were in a relationship before.

ADRIANA *touches his arm. He withdraws.*

I get back on Friday, we could meet on Saturday. You know? It will be nice we can just . . .

NICK. You should stay with your family.

ADRIANA. I should be here. Exactly. Let's meet, let's meet right here.

NICK. I can't. On Saturday.

ADRIANA. OK then, Sunday. Just . . . I promise you it will be different.

NICK. Look, we are friends, yeah, and we have this one, this big thing that we're both going through . . .

ADRIANA. I need your support.

NICK. That's why I brought you here, to get a bit of sunshine and to talk as friends and grown-ups and to make sure you are one-hundred-per-cent confident about getting on the plane.

ADRIANA. But I'm not sure I am.

NICK. Er, you were when we sat down moments ago, and –

ADRIANA. I want to know we'll have an after.

NICK. You'll get support at home. You've come from a / great –

ADRIANA. No no, I won't. They don't want to . . . they don't . . .

NICK. Well, your mum is going to look after you, you're her little girl.

ADRIANA. No.

Beat.

NICK. Look, afterwards you're not going to want to see me.

ADRIANA. Yes I will. How do you know what I want?

NICK. I've got a fairly clear idea, and . . .

ADRIANA. Please. I have to meet you.

NICK. Er, to do what, Adriana, basically?

ADRIANA. To talk. This is a big deal.

NICK. Let's talk now. Let's . . .

ADRIANA. No no no. I don't know how I'm going to feel afterwards. It's hard.

NICK. You're stronger than you think you are. You're stronger than me.

ADRIANA. I'm not. I want you to imagine it and I want you to go through this with me.

NICK. Well, I am going through it. My life has gone to shit.

ADRIANA. I can't do this without meeting afterwards.

NICK. You want me to be –

ADRIANA. Do you actually know what I'm doing?

NICK. – you want me to be a boyfriend / figure.

ADRIANA. No. I don't / want that.

NICK. I can't be that.

ADRIANA. You can't leave me to do all of this alone.

NICK. Do you understand?

ADRIANA (*losing it*). No, Nick. Do you? (*Beat.*) I want to show you something.

She looks in her bag.

NICK. What. What is it?

ADRIANA. See this?

She produces a pen from her bag.

NICK. Yeah.

ADRIANA. This is the size of our baby.

NICK. Oh can't . . . Jesus Christ.

ADRIANA. That's what I'm trying to make you understand.

NICK. I know, I understand. I'm not a fucking idiot.

ADRIANA. If you understand / how can you say –

NICK. You should be with your family.

ADRIANA. My family don't care. You're just trying to put me on the plane and get rid of me. I'm just trying to make you understand this is a big deal.

NICK. Believe me, I have a very, very good idea of . . .

ADRIANA. You will have your friends and you will have your girlfriend and I will have nobody.

NICK. I'm not good at looking after you.

ADRIANA. You are.

NICK. I can't do it.

Beat. ADRIANA *readies to leave.*

(*Quickly.*) Call me, then, if you want.

ADRIANA. Promise?

NICK. You promise me you'll do this.

ADRIANA. Yes, of course, I've told you I'd do it.

NICK. Why did you show me that . . .

ADRIANA. But I need to know that / you'll be –

NICK. I'll be there where you get back.

ADRIANA. Promise?

NICK. I wouldn't lie to you, Adriana. OK? You have my hundred-per-cent support.

ADRIANA. Promise?

NICK. I'll be there. I'll see you when you . . . I'll see you. We can talk . . .

ADRIANA. Promise?

NICK. Yeah. We'll go for a coffee, OK?

ADRIANA. You don't mean it.

NICK. Why do you say that?

ADRIANA. Because I can tell.

ADRIANA moves away, NICK takes her hand, caresses it and looks into her eyes.

NICK. Look, when you get back we'll sit down and have a coffee and we'll talk like two grown-ups. I promise you that. I've fucked up. But I'm not going to leave you on your own. You can rely on me. I care about you. I really do care. OK? OK?

ADRIANA. Then I will do it.

NICK. OK. OK. Good.

Long pause. They continue to try to read each other. NICK gives her a hug, which grows in sincerity. ADRIANA breaks away.

ADRIANA. I think you are a good person, Nick. I love you.

She leaves.

NICK. Call me when you're there too, if you want. You can always call me.

Blackout.

Scene Fourteen

August–April, the following year.

Snapshot No. 1, of NICK *slumped at home. He's trying to read the contents of a Pot Noodle.*

Snapshot No. 2, of ADRIANA *arriving back in the UK with her suitcase, making a mobile phone call and not getting an answer.*

NICK *gives his speech at* RICH*'s wedding.* RICH *and* LUCY *are present on stage, but the focus is solely on* NICK.

NICK (*reading from cards*). He is, quite simply, perfect. Now I hear a few sniggers amongst you. (*Breaks.*) Actually a few more than a few – but all forty of us there for Rich's stag weekend in (*Pointed.*) Venice Beach discussed this and all of you here, even those who have known Rich as long as I have, will have to admit, you have to rack your brains to work out how one person could, so truly, have it all. He's got the job with the income that makes your breathing go funny when you hear it, he's got the house in one of those North London streets the Americans use in their films, and now he's got Sarah. Frankly, it makes you sick, doesn't it? In all seriousness, to see the two as happy as this makes me more incredibly happy than I have ever admitted to Rich. Seeing your friend transformed by meeting a girl is an amazing experience. And I feel very privileged to have witnessed close up the wonderful change in Rich that happened when he met Caroline, er, Sarah. I think you'll agree with me . . . er, that right from the start they have appeared the perfect couple and it is no exaggeration to say that . . . that . . . Rich . . . I . . . think that Rich is . . . the most . . . I think you should all know . . . that . . . it's not how . . . it's not . . . none of this . . . it's all . . . going to . . . I'm going to . . . stop. Now.

NICK *walks away.*

Snapshot No. 3, of ADRIANA *on her bed, still in her flat under the Westway. She is putting the finishing touches to her make-up before determinedly heading out of her bedsit.*

Snapshot No. 4, of NICK *asleep with his laptop. It is night. He's been drinking. His flat's ever more untidy. We don't see the screen but he's been on the internet. JOE is standing over* NICK, *looking at the screen. He lifts the laptop off* NICK *and closes it up.*

Scene Fifteen

April 22nd.

Costa Coffee.

JOE. Hi.

LUCY. Hi.

JOE. How are you?

LUCY. All right.

JOE. Good.

LUCY. Loving the new job.

JOE. Yeah? MKPG, isn't it?

LUCY. Long hours, but the people are great, so . . .

JOE. Good. You . . . are you all ready for the wedding?

LUCY. Pretty much. Can't wait.

JOE. Yeah . . .

LUCY. And you'll get to meet Neil, so.

JOE. Yeah. How's that going?

LUCY. Great.

JOE. Good.

LUCY. How's the planning?

JOE. It's all right. It's all, you know . . . Look, I'll get to the point. Because it's kind of wedding-based. How are we going to have you and Nick at the centre of the whole thing with everything that happened . . . because it's a big mess.

LUCY. Yeah.

JOE. And the state of that man, in the last six months, it's just, he's got worse and worse and worse and you're the cause of it and yet somehow we've all got to be together on this big day which for Sophie and for me is like our biggest day there will ever be.

LUCY. Well, obviously it's crossed my mind and I think you should reconsider your best-man choice.

JOE. Reconsider my best man?

LUCY. Yes.

JOE. Lucy, I . . . I'm not . . .

LUCY. And I say that . . .

JOE. He is my best man, / right?

LUCY. Yeah, but . . .

JOE. So . . .

LUCY. Nick at Rich's wedding was –

JOE. Yeah, OK. At Rich's wedding his performance wasn't exactly the greatest, but what I want is to make it better and sort him out and then it's fine. I don't expect you to be dancing with each other but you don't have any right to tell me to re-choose my best man because it doesn't suit you.

LUCY. It's really not about me.

JOE. This is my day and Sophie's day.

LUCY. I know.

JOE. Well / it seems –

LUCY. I'm prepared to stand with Neil on the other side of the hall. I'm not going to make a scene, I've got more dignity than that.

JOE. Yes, but the trouble is –

LUCY. I will do / my job.

JOE. Nick might make a scene.

LUCY. Yes.

JOE. And it seems to me it's your fault that he's going to make a scene.

LUCY. No, it's noth . . . it's because he's . . .

JOE. Lucy, you walked out on him with no reasoning and you shattered him, the boy's heartbroken and no one knows why. You don't speak to Sophie about it. Nick won't speak to me about it – he just sits on his sofa drinking, watching daytime television. And he's just falling to pieces. And the only person I can think of who knows why that might have happened is you. And you won't talk about it. Do you understand how hurtful it is to me and Sophie to be in the middle of it?

LUCY. What the fuck?

JOE. I appreciate . . .

LUCY. I'm sorry the breaking-up of my relationship has been hurtful to you and Sophie.

JOE. Look, I appreciate that there's something deeply . . .

LUCY. Don't be a cock, Joe.

JOE. Look, my oldest friend has had his life destroyed by whatever happened between the two of you. And if I knew, I could help him. All I want to do is help him.

LUCY. Why haven't you asked him?

JOE. I've asked him over and over again for six months.

LUCY. Well, do you wonder why he doesn't tell you?

JOE. I don't know why he wouldn't tell me, but it's obviously something very important . . . I think he needs to speak to you. Something has to be cleared up.

LUCY. I'm not seeing him. He's not . . .

JOE. But you're going to see him at the wedding.

LUCY. Yeah, but I don't have to talk to him.

JOE. Oh for fuck's sake . . .

LUCY. Joe, I think . . .

JOE. Look, you owe him at least / some sort of –

LUCY. I owe him nothing. Excuse me, I owe him nothing.

JOE. Look, you just turned off this relationship.

LUCY. I did not.

JOE. It's how it looks to me.

LUCY. You have no idea.

JOE. Well, no, I don't and maybe I'm here trying to find out. Because something has to give. We can't all live in the dark about this any more. All I know is that one day you were happy, you were going out, and I've never seen him happier and that was six months ago, and since then he's just been a shadow and the only person I can blame is you, because I know there's no way he would want to split up with you, 'cause I know him that well.

LUCY. You know him / that well.

JOE. And I know that he can't cope without you.

LUCY. You know him so well.

JOE. Yeah, I do, I know him very well. I've known him since / we were . . .

LUCY. He was having an affair.

JOE. Oh, don't start throwing out random accusations.

LUCY. Fine. Fine.

Beat.

JOE. Right, who was he having an affair with? Who who who was this person that I know nothing about, that he was running around with?

LUCY. Some Italian girl that he got pregnant.

Beat.

JOE. No. I. No. I don't believe you. I . . . because. . . . if . . . if Nick was having an affair with an Italian girl when he was going out with you, I'm sorry to say I would have known about it. And and . . .

LUCY. Joe, you wouldn't.

JOE. I would have tried to stop it.

LUCY. Joe, what the fuck's wrong with you? I would have known about it. I mean, it did happen but I didn't know about it, so therefore you couldn't have known about it. That's not the lie. He fooled me.

JOE. I don't believe you.

LUCY. And he was supposedly in love with me.

JOE. He was in love with you. That's the thing. That's exactly my point, he wouldn't . . .

LUCY. That's absolute bollocks.

JOE. He wouldn't have an affair –

LUCY. Joe.

JOE. – behind your back. I saw you two together, and I saw him . . .

LUCY. Joe, I heard it on the answerphone, he admitted it, he confessed, we rowed about it, it broke us up. He can't tell you because he's . . .

JOE. This is . . . honestly? You promise me this is why?

LUCY. I'm not malicious, Joe. I'm sorry.

JOE. Er. He wouldn't, he wouldn't lie to me for six months.

LUCY. He wouldn't lie to me for four months apparently, but he did. Joe. He's not the man you think he is.

JOE. But hang on, no. No, I don't believe you. Because you would have told Sophie this and Sophie would have told me because there's no way my future wife . . .

LUCY. Sophie's shown she's not great with sensitive information, all right? (*Pause.*) I'm sorry to be the one who breaks this to you, but Nick has this dark side. He's a liar and he can't be trusted.

JOE. He's the devil.

LUCY. He's not the devil, he just can't be trusted. It's about honesty.

JOE. Honesty. He only found out about you and kids because Sophie told me.

LUCY. What? Joe, I wasn't being dishonest, I just hadn't told him yet.

JOE. If this is true, it's no wonder he was trying to screw someone else.

LUCY. What the hell do you mean?

JOE. I mean that talking about honesty is a bit rich coming from you.

LUCY. You're saying that he got someone else pregnant because he found out later I might not have kids? What?

JOE. I don't know what I mean, all right?

Beat.

I need to speak to Nick. Until I speak to him and look him in the eye and he tells me what the fucking hell this is all about, I'm not . . .

LUCY. Fine.

LUCY *readies to leave*.

JOE. Lucy, for the wedding . . . Look, can you . . . He just needs some sort of contact . . .

LUCY. Joe. I owe him absolutely nothing so don't ask me to sort him out.

JOE. What are you going to do?

LUCY. I've got to go.

JOE. Lucy. What are you going to do at the wedding?

LUCY. I'm going to smile sweetly. (*Beat.*) Just ask him about Adriana.

Blackout.

Scene Sixteen

April 22nd. Later the same day.

Evening. NICK's flat. A football match plays on the TV. Both NICK and the flat are a greater mess than before. NICK slumps on the sofa. The doorbell rings. It's JOE.

NICK. Hello, fella, come on in. Come on in. Beer?

JOE. No, thanks.

NICK. Sit down. It's Chelsea. Hey. I looked into the champagne and I've basically sorted it.

JOE. Yeah?

NICK. It all comes down to how good you want to look. So. Your Moët's a reasonable £14 a bottle. But pretty shit. Your Bollinger's a rather scary £35 a throw, but will be noticed. Or for laughs, you could go down the Asda Cava route and lose friends.

JOE. All sounds good.

NICK. Ten crates of Bolly it is, then. Hey, you spoken to Soph?

JOE. When?

NICK. About the invitations?

JOE. They've gone.

NICK. She's sent the one to Lucy?

JOE. Yeah.

NICK. Just to Lucy. Not to Investment Banker.

JOE. Neil.

NICK. Yeah.

JOE. Neil's coming.

Beat.

NICK. I think, I thought I'd be straight with you. I don't want Investment Banker coming. I think to give you a good speech and stuff it's best that Investment Banker isn't there. So how do you feel about that?

JOE. I understand that.

NICK. I'm glad you said that. I feel bad about that. So how are you?

JOE. I bumped into Lucy actually. Down at Costa.

NICK. Ah.

JOE. She, she told me some things. About her and you.

NICK. It's all in the past.

JOE. It's not really in the past, is it?

NICK. Truly.

JOE. Look at this flat. And you're looking good, mate.

NICK. So what did she say, then?

JOE. She was just telling me what happened with you two.

NICK. God. Poor you.

JOE. Nick. What happened?

NICK. I don't know.

JOE. Nick.

NICK. Who knows? Don't listen to what she told you.

JOE. Nick. I asked to see Lucy.

NICK. No you didn't.

JOE. I didn't like to see you like this. I asked to see her to see if I could get anything from her about you.

NICK. Joe. There's nothing wrong. The cleaner just didn't have a visa, that's all. You've broken the code. I can't believe you asked to see Lucy. You shouldn't have done that.

JOE. Broken the code, yeah. We wouldn't want to do that.

NICK. What. What. What's the problem? I'm sorting shit out for you and you're going off having coffee with . . .

JOE. There's nothing wrong with you?

Beat.

NICK. No.

Beat.

JOE. Look, I've asked you this before but now . . . I want you to be my best man, but I need you to be absolutely open with me.

NICK. I've been completely open with you.

JOE. About Lucy?

NICK. Yeah.

JOE. Really?

NICK. What did she say?

JOE. Who the fuck is Adriana?

NICK. I don't know. Who the fuck *is* Adriana? The cleaner? Who is Adriana?

JOE. . . .

NICK. What did she tell you? What did she say exactly exactly exactly?

JOE. . . .

NICK. Oh, so that's right. So you think that despite the ten-year friendship between us she's going to walk in and persuade you that I'm actually a dick and that I'm going to lie to you and all this because I'm fucking . . . fat? What kind of loyalty is that?

JOE. Why didn't you tell me?

NICK. What. Tell you that I had a one-night stand? I had a one-night stand.

JOE. You had a one-night stand. OK. But you didn't tell me.

NICK. I didn't think it was important.

JOE (*angry*). I've been looking after you for six months since you broke up. Why the fuck didn't you think that was important, Nick? Why didn't you think it would help me to know what happened? I want the whole truth and I fucking deserve it.

NICK. I had a one-night stand. It's not a dumpable offence. Going out with Neil the Banker, now that's a dumpable offence. I want to be your best man.

JOE. I want you to be my best man. Who is Adriana?

NICK. Who is Adriana? Was that her name?

JOE. Why didn't you tell me?

NICK. Because, because, I ... because ... it wasn't ... very ... nice.

JOE. Did anything else happen with her?

NICK. No. Sorry, I don't know anything more about her.

JOE. Look, I'm just going to ask you this. Did you get this girl pregnant?

NICK. No.

JOE. Did you?

NICK. No.

JOE. It's fine either way. Honestly. I really don't mind. But I need to trust you, Nick.

NICK. I'm yours. I'm an open book.

JOE. Yeah?

NICK. Yeah.

JOE. OK. (*Squarely.*) If you're lying to me, you're a cunt.

NICK. I'm not.

JOE (*relieved*). OK. Good.

NICK. Can I still be your best man?

JOE. God, you need this, don't you?

Blackout.

Scene Seventeen

July 16th. Three months later.

JOE*'s stag night.* NICK*'s flat. As they were at the start of the play,* NICK *and* JOE *are dressing.* NICK *is in his boxer shorts.*

NICK (*pumped up*). So what are the rules of the game? I intend to catch a sexually-transmitted disease tonight. What about you?

JOE. I am going to get drunk, get you laid and wake up in a police cell.

NICK. And what about girls for you? What about kissing? Is kissing one on the mouth OK?

JOE. No.

NICK. Shoulder?

JOE. Yes.

NICK. Nose?

JOE. Yes.

NICK. Mouth?

JOE. No.

NICK. Oh, what's the difference between nose and mouth? OK, so the last person in the world you're going to sleep with is Sophie. That's fine. But suppose tonight Scarlett Johansson came up to you and said, 'Joe, I've heard you've got a huge schlonger.' How about it? Foxhunting's worse, surely.

JOE. All right, one last dalliance. For Scarlett's sake. She needs it.

NICK. Hooray. Thank fuck for that. That's on the record, by the way. I'm putting it in the speech.

JOE. Yeah, I wanted to talk about the speech.

NICK. Me too. Listen, I've sent out a lot of e-mails to lots of people asking for stories and got some answers that frankly I don't think are legal.

JOE. You're joking.

NICK. Yes.

JOE. Look, I want to talk about the speech, but I can't when you're being like this.

NICK. Joe. It's your fucking *stag night*. They're coming in twenty minutes.

JOE. Just tread carefully.

NICK. Relax. You didn't see the best-man speech Rich got. I should have sent you a copy. It was a beautiful thing. I'll make yours a bit more filthy, but there's nothing for you to worry about.

JOE. I'm getting married, Nick. There'll be friends and Sophie's family. I'm / getting fucking married.

NICK. You're getting fucking married. / It's fine. I'll add some well-judged stuff about the bridesmaid's past, your past, Sophie's past, I'm joking.

JOE. I'm not sure we're on the same wavelength here.

NICK. OK. OK. So here's a pen. What don't you want me to say?

JOE. I just don't want you to talk about . . . the person I was.

NICK. I'll do what you say, but no one's going to buy it. Half of the people in the marquee will have slept with you. Neil the Banker's probably slept with you. You know, when I meet him I'm going to go up to him, shake his hand, look him in the eye and go 'Blaaaaghh!!' Oh, there's news. I've met a girl.

JOE. Yeah?

NICK. Well, I haven't met her, but I've seen her, I've seen a photo of her and she . . .

JOE. You're not internet dating?

NICK. Yeah, it's fine.

JOE (*laughs*). No, it's not fine.

NICK. No, wait, hear me out. She is, she is absolutely fucking stunning, she has a perfect – assuming it's her photo – a perfect . . .

JOE (*in hysterics*). Oh my God. You're going to meet some fat old . . .

NICK. No, her name is . . . No no. Wait for this . . .

JOE. No, please stop. This is hurting and –

NICK. Don't mock my future.

JOE. Oww!

NICK. I'm going to sleep with this girl.

JOE. I'm not going to allow you to.

NICK. Her name is Fallen Angel. Fallen Angel, I'm going to sleep with Fallen Angel, Fallen Angel, Fallen Angel, full carnal knowledge, bring it on, I have a photo.

JOE. I want to see this.

NICK. Let me get the photo. Don't play with yourself when I show it to you.

JOE. It's very unlikely.

NICK. I feel strongly about this girl . . .

JOE. Oh God. Let me find you a real woman.

NICK. She is a real woman, she's a real, hot-blooded . . . she's perfect. Apparently in relationships we're ninety-two per cent compatible. And I'm only seventy-seven per cent compatible with myself.

NICK *exits to get the photo. There's a knock at the door.* JOE *looks around. Another knock.*

JOE. Nick?

No answer. JOE *opens the door.* ADRIANA *is standing on the porch holding a baby. They don't recognise each other from their brief Tube encounter . . .*

ADRIANA. Can I speak to Nick?

JOE. Er, yeah. Come in.

ADRIANA. Thank you.

ADRIANA *walks into the house and sits down on the sofa.*

JOE. He's just in the other room getting a . . . Boy?

ADRIANA. Girl.

JOE (*looks at baby*). She's cute.

Pause.

Sorry, have we . . . [met]?

ADRIANA. I don't think so.

JOE. No. Do you want to sit down?

ADRIANA. No, I'm OK. I'm not going to stay.

JOE. What's your name?

ADRIANA. I'm Adriana.

JOE. Adriana. (*Beat.*) Right, OK. Er, Nick.

NICK (*offstage*). Yeah, yeah, no, I've nearly got it, nearly got it.

JOE. No, I think just forget the photo.

NICK (*offstage*). No, I'll be there in a minute, mate.

JOE. Come here now.

NICK (*offstage*). Gorgeous, tits to die for.

JOE. Do you . . . Are you from . . .

ADRIANA. I'm a friend of Nick's.

JOE. But where are you from originally?

ADRIANA. From Italy.

JOE. I see. Nick!

NICK (*offstage*). No, no, I've got it. I've got it.

JOE. Really fucking hurry up.

NICK. I've got it. Gorgeous fucking . . .

NICK in, holding the photo.

JOE. Adriana.

ADRIANA and NICK hold a gaze. Then she looks down at the baby. Happy. Radiant.

A pause.

NICK. Everything OK?

ADRIANA. Me or the baby?

NICK. The baby. Both of you.

ADRIANA. Perfect.

Beat.

NICK. Boy?

JOE. It's a girl.

NICK. What's her name?

ADRIANA. Gabriella.

NICK. That's a beautiful name.

JOE. I'll go and . . . make a cup of tea.

NICK. Yeah. Tea would be nice.

JOE. Adriana?

ADRIANA. No thanks.

NICK. Thanks, mate.

JOE *goes into the kitchen, slamming the door behind him.*

ADRIANA. Hi. How are you?

NICK. Er. How are you?

ADRIANA. I'm good. You look different.

NICK. Wow, so do you, you look great.

ADRIANA. Thank you. I just wanted to see you. I go back to Italy tomorrow. And I just wanted to see how you were.

NICK. Well, good, yeah, good. Joe and I are sort of heading out.

ADRIANA. OK, I'm not going to stay, I've got a taxi waiting, I just –

NICK. It's really good to see you, actually.

ADRIANA. It's good to see you.

NICK. I should have phoned. I'm sorry.

ADRIANA. It's OK. I found where you lived. I could have come sooner but . . .

Beat.

You want to see?

She brings Gabriella over.

Bella.

NICK *tries to hold himself together as he looks.*

NICK. God, I'm sorry. She's beautiful. I'm sorry. Pathetic.

ADRIANA. It's OK.

NICK. I'm really sorry.

ADRIANA. It's OK.

NICK. She's . . . she's lovely. Can I hold her?

ADRIANA. OK.

She hands her over to NICK.

NICK. She's tiny. She's tiny.

NICK *holds her. Relaxed, long beat.*

Good.

ADRIANA. I'm a mama.

NICK. Yeah, congratulations on that. I did sometimes wonder if I was a dad, you know, in Caffè Nero sometimes with the accents and the music, I had these pictures in my head. Wow. What, just, well, tell me what happened? You went back to Italy and . . .

ADRIANA. And I had the abortion. Like I said I would.

NICK *freezes.* ADRIANA *notices.*

And then I came back about, er, a week later and that's when when your phone wasn't working. (*Beat.*) I was getting the tone, then about one month later I met someone, and then and then Gabriella came.

NICK *hands back Gabriella, clearly upset.*

NICK. Wow.

ADRIANA. I'm sorry. I didn't think you would think . . .

NICK. No. Er, we should, we should, we should actually . . .

ADRIANA. But I hope I hope that you find this one day.

NICK. Well, that's . . . I'll be fine.

ADRIANA. Because I just want you to be happy.

NICK. Er, thank you.

ADRIANA. That's why I came. That's what I wanted you to –

A beat as ADRIANA *tries to convey it all in words.*

JOE *comes in.*

JOE. Tea's on its way. So is the dad Italian?

ADRIANA. No, no, he's English, I don't see him.

JOE. So he's all right with you taking his baby? That's . . .

NICK. It's really . . . thank you so much for coming. It's been absolutely lovely to see you and, you know, good luck and if there's anything I can do . . .

ADRIANA *shakes her head.*

ADRIANA. No, I'm not going to come back.

NICK. No, OK, but if there's anything, just send me an e-mail.

ADRIANA *shakes her head again.*

ADRIANA. Goodbye.

NICK. Thank you.

JOE. Nice to meet you.

NICK. Take care of yourself.

ADRIANA *leaves.*

Good. Good. OK. So let's go, pal. Want a drink? A proper drink?

JOE. No.

NICK. Want to talk about about the plan? Want to see Fallen Angel?

JOE. No.

NICK. Not my baby.

JOE. So it was all shit.

NICK. Not my baby.

JOE. All shit.

NICK. No. It wasn't shit.

JOE. You lying, lying bastard.

NICK. That wasn't my baby. That's the God's honest truth.

JOE. You have no fucking respect.

NICK. But it wasn't my baby. It wasn't my baby.

JOE. You swore you had . . .

NICK (*erupts*). I slept with her *once* when I'd just started going out with Lucy! That's it! That's all I did! I fucked up ONCE! Have you never done anything like that? You look me in the eye, Joe Rickett, and tell me you haven't done anything like that.

Beat.

JOE. What *have* you done?

NICK. Joe.

Silence.

JOE (*avoiding eye-contact*). I don't want you on the stag.

NICK. Why would you do that?

JOE. I don't want you at the wedding either.

NICK. I'm your best man. You're my best friend.

JOE. Yeah. See ya.

JOE *exits.* NICK *alone. The light fades slowly to a final blackout.*

The End.